THE UNKNOWN COMMANDANT

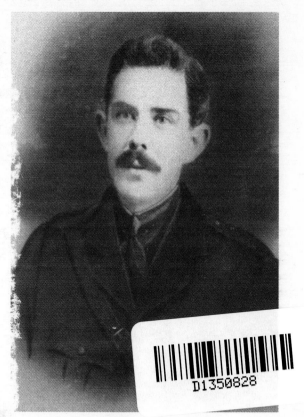

Commandant Denis Barry
Brigade Staff
Cork No. 1 Brigade Óglaigh na h-Éireann
1883–1923

Flag of the Cork Brigade of the Irish Volunteers. (Courtesy of the Cork City Museum)

Denis Barry is a retired industrial manager who has always had a keen interest in politics, history and sport. A nephew of the book's subject, he is passionate about the largely forgotten history of many of our patriots. This project began innocently enough in a graveyard and turned into a labour of love.

THE UNKNOWN COMMANDANT

The Life and Times of Denis Barry 1883–1923

Denis Barry

The Collins Press

FIRST PUBLISHED IN 2010 BY
The Collins Press
West Link Park
Doughcloyne
Wilton
Cork

British Library Cataloguing in Publication Data
Barry, Denis.
    The unknown commandant : the life and times of Denis
Barry
    1883-1923.
    1. Barry, Denis. 2. Guerrillas–Ireland–Biography.
    3. Political prisoners–Ireland–Biography.
    I. Title
    941.7'082'092-dc22
    ISBN-13: 9781848890299

Typesetting by The Collins Press
Typeset in Goudy 11.5 pt
Printed in Great Britan by J F Print Ltd

Cover photos
Front (main): Denis Barry (*Barry family archive*)
Front and back: (background) Cork city after being burnt in 1920 (*Barry
family archive*); l–r: troops leaving Victoria Barracks (*Osprey*), the 1909
and 1910 Blackrock hurling teams (*Blackrock Hurling Club*).

Contents

List of Appendices

This book is dedicated to the memory of
Commandant Denis Barry 1883–1923
Brigade Staff – Cork No. 1 Brigade, Óglaigh na hÉireann
1914–1922
and
Divisional Staff – 3rd Eastern Brigade Wexford, 1922

Also in memory of all the officers and volunteers who fought in
our War of Independence – some of whom have, sadly, been
forgotten – and members of Cumann na mBan who took part
in active service, and those who provided care and shelter for
their own and those who were engaged in the final push to rid
our country of the occupying force.

Reamhrá

Timpeall cúig bhliana ó shin agus mé ar cuairt ar Reilig Fhionnbharra Naofa i gCorcaigh bhíos i mo sheasamh os comhair uaigh m'uncail, Donnchadh de Barra. Tháinig fear taobh liom agus d'fhiafraigh sé díom cérbh é an fear san.

D'inneas scéal a bheatha dó, ach níor mhór an t-eolas a bhí agam le tabhairt dó.

Ar fhilleadh abhaile dhom, thainig náire orm i dtaobh a laghad eolais a bhí agam ar m'uncail.

Shocraíos an lá san go ndhéanfainn mo dhícheall chun scéal Dhonnchaidh a chur le chéile. Ní raibh radharc na súl ar fónamh agam, ach bhraitheas mar sin féin go raibh dualgas orm an leabhar seo a scríobh. Thugas cuairt ar Iarsmalann Chorcaí agus ar Leabharlanna Chorcaí agus fuaireas blúirí eolais.

Diaidh ar ndiaidh bhí an pictiúr ag teacht le chéile. Bhí a thuilleadh eolais le fáil agam i seanpháipeirí nuachta agus ó Chumainn Iománaíochta Bhaile an Mhairtéalaigh

The Unknown Commandant

agus na Carraige Duibhe. Bhí a thuilleadh páipéar le fáil i Leabharlann Chill Chainnigh freisin. Le cabhair óna lán daoine is ea cuireadh an scéal so le chéile. Mheasas gurbh iomchuí an brollach so a scriobh i nGaeilge in omós Dhonnchadh.

(Aistrithe ag Liam P. Ó Murchú, Roinn na Gaeilge, UCC)

Preface

About five years ago when I was visiting my parents' grave in St Finbarr's Cemetery, Glasheen Road, Cork, I paused at the Republican Plot near the entrance to the cemetery. As I stood there, reading the plaques on the three grave mounds at the front of the Plot, a man nearby said to me, 'Do you know anything about that man', pointing at the mound on the left. 'I know about Terence MacSwiney and Tomás MacCurtain but I never heard anything about him.' He was referring to my uncle and namesake, Denis Barry, who was buried there in November 1923, having died in Newbridge Internment Camp after spending thirty-five days on hunger strike.

I told my inquirer as best I could about Denis and how he came to be buried in such a prominent position, but my knowledge was limited and sketchy and largely gleaned from stories told to me as a child by my elders.

When I returned home and reflected on what had transpired, I felt a certain shame that I did not know more about my uncle and his life and times. I resolved there and then to do something about it. I paid visits to the Cork Public Museum, Cork City Library and Cork Archives and found some information. More information was available in old newspapers and from the records of Ballymartle and Blackrock Hurling Clubs. From Kilkenny Library yet more information was received. Piece by piece a picture began to emerge. This little book is the result. I trust it will stand as a modest tribute to a man who played his full part in the fight for Irish freedom but about whom very little is written in the history books.

Acknowledgements

The author is deeply grateful for the help of the following people without whose assistance the project could not have been completed: Michael Higgins, Tim, Brian and the other staff at Cork City Archives, Great William O'Brien Street, Blackpool; Dan Breen and assistants at Cork Public Museum, Fitzgeralds Park; all those at Cork City Library who helped in any way, particularly the staff in the Reference Section and in the Cork Local History Department; all at the *Irish Examiner* for their help and for permission to use both text and photographs; Damien Brett, Kilkenny County Library, for his help in locating newspapers for 1916–1923; Tom O'Sullivan of Blackrock Hurling Club for information, match reports and photographs; Mr E. Kelly and Mr Bob O'Regan of Ballymartle Hurling Club; Rev. Tomás Ó Murchú, Sagart Paróiste, Áth an Mhaide; Brian Ó Mhuirthle, Séamus Ó Lionacháin, Liam P. Ó Murchú agus Criostóir de Baróid a thug cabhair mhór dhom agus Pádraig Ó Cúanacháin RIP, a thug misneach dom nuair a bhí an spriod lag agam.

The Unknown Commandant

Sincere thanks to my wife, Patsy, for her help and patience during the long days of research; to my two sons, Donagh and Emmet, for all their encouragement after a period of doubt about the book, to my nieces, Fiona and Celine, for their interest and encouragement; to my brother-in-law, John O'Mahony, who helped with procuring newspapers and books in Dublin; to Gerry White, co-author of *Baptised in Blood: The Formation of the Cork Brigade of the Irish Volunteers 1913–1916* and *The Burning of Cork* and to Ross O' Sullivan M.A. for all his help and advice.

Last but not least I would like to thank all my friends at the Low Vision Centre of the National Council of the Blind in Ireland whose assistance, training and guidance was a major factor in my ability to cope with glaucoma. In particular I would like to mention Brian Manning, who, though blind from birth, instructed me on the use of a computer and other aids needed.

Foreword

As we get nearer to the 100th anniversary of 1916 there is increasing interest in understanding the events that led to our freedom, and the foundation of our political institutions. Because it very much characterises who we are as a nation amongst the nations of the world it us understandable why this part of Irish history should be analysed, discussed, reviewed, reflected on, and celebrated.

However, writing history is difficult because the people who do so, whether they be professional or amateur historians, or writing family memoirs, bring their own personal and political biases to the task. Also, it is about resolving differing personal accounts about events that happened very quickly and under great stress.

As we all know, the Civil War overshadowed the War of Independence. Comrades became opponents, leaders died in suspicious circumstances, stories were told about people that only partially reflected the truth, and, in some cases, the stories were not told at all. This book is about one of these, Denis Barry, whose story is told here for the first time.

There are so many unanswered questions about this time, and so many stories yet unwritten. There is no authoritative history of the Irish Republican Police, of which Denis Barry was the first commandant in Cork. There is not even an authoritative history of the Irish Republican Brotherhood (IRB) during that critical time after Dáil Éireann had instituted its own government in January 1919. There has been no detailed study of the role of the IRB at a local level throughout the War of Independence, in terms of the chain of command in the army. What were the relationships between people who apparently had so much in common from early on and for so long, and ended up so far apart, as happened between Denis Barry and Dick Mulcahy, both senior members of the Volunteers from Munster who were interned together in Frongoch? One view is that 'going over old ground' will be not a pretty sight, and will lead to family upsets. This was my father's view. But that was some time ago when many of the following generation were still living, which is no longer the case.

'Nature abhors a vacuum.' We are faced now with the travesty where some Revisionist historians are trying to take what is known to be true and prove that 'white is black', i.e. to destroy the reputations of great heroes through selective joining together of unrepresentative reports. All historians should be revisionists (with a small 'r'), i.e. constantly uncovering more evidence and refining what is known so as to get deeper insights into historical events. The challenge is how to respond to people who bring to their interest in history an emotionally based position that colours what they select to use as evidence and how to put it together into a story of the events. Our response to this challenge can only be to fight for the truth, even if it hurts some people.

People's fears in this regard have been exaggerated. The people who carried the burden of the War of Independence were great men and women. When they started the expectations were so low that 'fellow travellers' and opportunists did not join. If some of these people did or said wrong things later, such as in the Civil War, there probably were reasons, in hindsight, not justifications. Now is the time to try to understand them, neither to condemn them nor to 'sweep them under the carpet'.

In this biography of his uncle, Denis Barry has done a service to his namesake, to his family, and to us, because this is a story that had not been told, and that needed to be told. Denis (Denny) Barry holds the title of commandant because he was one of the officers on the Brigade Staff of the Cork No.1 Brigade of Óglaigh na hÉireann between 1914 and 1922, and also because he was Commandant of the Republican Police in Cork during the War of Independence. This was a significant position because he had to contend with the deterioration in the behaviour of the British forces in Cork city, the army, auxiliaries, black and tans, and RIC.

Some things make this story special, or at least unusual. The first is why Denis Barry should be described as the 'Unknown Commandant'. Until recently the Department of Defence had not formally recognised Denis Barry's involvement in the War of Independence. As

The Unknown Commandant

Denis had died in 1923, he had not sought a Military Service Pension or a Service Medal. Therefore there were no personal details of his participation in the War of Independence in official departmental records. Nonetheless, following a request from his nephew, the Department carried out a search of its records and found sufficient evidence to justify the posthumous award of a Service (1917–1921) Medal to Denis Barry.

Other reasons why he remained unknown were because he moved to Kilkenny in 1915, and so was not part of the main action in Cork, and because of the death of his commanding officers on the Cork No.1 Brigade staff, Lord Mayors MacCurtain and MacSwiney who, under normal circumstances, would have testified to his role.

Great credit is due to the author for doing so much to ensure proper recognition for his uncle.

As a person Denis was significant and interesting in other ways. He was an excellent hurler, particularly successful as a defender, and might nowadays have played the game at the highest level. The story that emerges in this book is of a defender not just in sport, but of citizens as Head of the Republican Police in Cork, as an active member of his trade union, but also in the role that led to his death. The treatment of prisoners in the internment camp in Newbridge, County Kildare, was very poor. Denis acted to help his fellow prisoners who were suffering inhumane treatment, using the only recourse which he felt open to him, protest by hunger strike.

The final reason why this story needs telling is to try to explain to future generations – and indeed to today's – why such an important person as Denny Barry was treated so

Foreword

badly at the end of his life, and after it. One part, which might seem explainable, is the behaviour the Free State Government who gave the impression that making any allowance would amount to giving the impression of weakness, which might in turn lead to more Republican resistance. The other part was the refusal by the Bishop of Cork to allow Barry's remains into any church in the Cork diocese, nor allow any priest to officiate at any religious funeral ceremony for him. This takes a lot more explaining, especially for young people nowadays. First, one must understand the power that bishops had then over civil affairs, and consequently their belief that they should use this power during political disputes. Bishop Daniel Coholan's actions contrast totally with his regarding MacSwiney, who had died on hunger strike only three years earlier.

It is a matter of pride for me that my two grand-aunts, Mary and Annie MacSwiney, participated in the burial ceremony at the grave, with Annie reciting the rosary in Irish, and Máire MacSwiney TD delivering the oration.

I welcome this book, and wish that others would follow the author's example, and help to contribute to a telling of the history of these brave men and women.

Prof. Cathal MacSwiney Brugha
University College Dublin
January 2010

Denis Barry was awarded posthumous service medal no. 1381 in December 2009 by the Department of Defence. (Barry family archive)

Introduction

Civil War in Ireland began in June 1922 with the Free State Government bombarding the Four Courts. After two days the anti-treaty forces surrendered and most of them dispersed around the country leaving the Free State Government in total control of Dublin. Free State forces increased from 14,000 in August 1922 to an unprecedented 55,000 some six months later.

The war dragged on around the country for another ten months until 30 April 1923 when Frank Aiken, the new IRA Chief of Staff, called a halt to what at that stage seemed a futile struggle. He issued an order for all Volunteers to dump arms rather than surrender. Thousands of anti-treaty IRA members, including most of its leaders still left alive, were arrested by Free State forces in the weeks following when they had dumped their arms and returned to their homes. Almost 12,000 Republicans were interned by the end of the Civil War, most of whom were not to be released until 1924. In October 1923 as many as 8,000 of these went on hunger strike to protest at the conditions under which they were being held and against their continued detention without charge or trial.

On Saturday 17 November 1923 a telegram was delivered to a farmhouse in Cullen, Riverstick, in south-east Cork. The message read: 'Your brother is now seriously ill in Newbridge Internment Camp, Co. Kildare. Every facility will be given to his family to visit him on making personal application to the Governor.' Batt Barry left immediately to travel the 140 miles to Newbridge. On his arrival he met the Military Governor, Seán Hayes, who escorted him to a hut where he saw his brother and three other men lying on stretcher beds on a dirty floor. His brother was conscious when Batt saw him but could not speak. He made an effort but went into convulsions. A doctor was sent for and Batt had to leave.

On Sunday 18 November Batt again visited his brother. He told the doctor in attendance that, in order to sustain his life, his brother should receive suitable treatment, including food, and should be sent to a hospital. Batt sent a telegram to the Minister for Defence, Richard Mulcahy, asking that his seriously ill brother be removed to a nursing home, since his case was hopeless. The response from the Minister was a firm 'no'.

On Monday 19 November a military ambulance left the Newbridge Internment Camp with a Republican officer on a stretcher, accompanied by a military doctor. The ambulance was on its way to the Curragh Military Hospital. The patient on the stretcher was a Brigade

Introduction

Commandant of the Cork No. 1 Brigade. His name was Denis Barry.

What follows is based on family papers, national and local newspapers of the day and other authentic documents. There did not exist among the latter a medal certificate awarded by the Department of Defence to those who participated in the War of Independence 1916–1921. The Military Records Office in Renmore, County Galway, have no record of Denis Barry, hence the book title, *The Unknown Commandant*.

The response from Military Archives, Rathmines, Dublin (see Appendix 9) initially suggested that record-keeping was not their forte. On 4 December 2009, the Department of Defence awarded a posthumous service medal to Denis Barry for service from 1917 to 1921.

Denis A. Barry
February 2010

1

Beginnings

Denis Barry was born on 13 July 1883 in the family home of his parents, John and Hanora Barry (née Sullivan), in Cullen, Riverstick, County Cork. His birth was registered in the district of Ballymartle at the Superintendent Registrar's District of Kinsale. The family farm where Denis was born was large by the standards of the time, being some 100 acres of the best arable land in the area. Part of the farm stretched up to the top of Cullen from where, on a clear night, Denis would have been able to see the lights of the Old Head of Kinsale lighthouse and also those of the town of Cobh, then called Queenstown. Like most farmers in those days, the Barrys were practically self-sufficient, the farm providing most of the necessities for life. They grew their own vegetables, kept a herd of cows that provided them

The Unknown Commandant

with a steady supply of milk, and also had pigs, chickens and ducks. They made their own butter and any surplus together with eggs would have been sold to Kennefick's Provision Shop in Barrack Street, Cork. This shop was also the source of general provisions, which were delivered to Cullen on a weekly basis.

The love of their faith and spoken Irish was at the heart of life on the farm. The family rosary was recited each night with all the family present. This practice lasted up to the late 1950s during which time the author used to spend his entire summer school holidays on the farm. The fields were each identified by an Irish name, e.g. Páirc Fada, Lios na Sí, and individual cows had names in Irish long before eartags became the norm. The issues of the War of Independence were never discussed in my presence and any questions would be politely answered by 'fadó, fadó'.

The Barry family was a large one. An extract from the census of Ireland 1901 shows the following details:

Name	Status	Age	Languages
John Barry	Head of family	78	Gaeilge/English
Nora Barry	Wife	57	Gaeilge/English
Nora Barry	Daughter	29	Gaeilge/English
Patrick Barry	Son	25	Gaeilge/English
Maggie Barry	Daughter	21	Gaeilge/English
John Barry	Son	19	Gaeilge/English
Michael Barry	Son	18	Gaeilge/English
Denis Barry	Son	16	Gaeilge/English
Batt Barry	Son	14	Gaeilge/English

Beginnings

Another daughter Catherine (Kate) Barry, aged twenty-seven, who was not in the house on census night, married a man called Donoghue and went to live in 25 Barrack Street, Cork.

Michael Barry, father of the author, is shown on the census form as 'Clerk'. Both Denis and Batt were registered as 'Scholars' on the form.

Patrick, the eldest son, emigrated to America some time between 1901 and 1911 and nothing further is known about him. Nora, who remained single, remained at home and worked hard throughout her life, carrying out the usual farm tasks.

Margaret (Maggie) married Walter Dain and reared three children: Walter, Joseph (Joe) and Olive. The families of Walter and Joe live in Dublin.

John (known as Jack) was involved in the War of Independence and afterwards managed the farm. He suffered from arthritis and spent the final long years of his life in severe pain, more or less confined to bed.

Batt joined the Ballinadee Company of the Volunteers and also took part in the War of Independence. He married Mary (Baby) O'Leary from nearby Glinny. They had no family. Batt and Baby also lived on the farm and survived Jack and Nora, Baby tending to her parents-in-law during their declining years. She was one of the most kind-hearted people that I have known in my lifetime and she helped to support my mother when my father, Michael, died in 1952, leaving her with four young children to provide for.

There was plenty of work for young Denis and his siblings to do. From an early age Denis would have had to help with a wide variety of farm chores, such as feeding poultry, milking cows, and helping with the harvest. Healthy competition was encouraged and a treat for the best worker of the day during harvest time would be a duck egg for lunch.

Denis began his education at the age of six in Ballymartle National School. At that time Ireland was experiencing what later became known as the 'Gaelic Revival' that saw the formation of the Gaelic League, the Gaelic Athletic Association and a renewed interest in all things Irish. John and Nora Barry shared this interest and passed it on to their children. Irish language and history were taught to all pupils of Ballymartle School in the 1890s and within a short time Denis displayed a keen interest in these subjects. His eagerness to learn led to his teacher, a Mr O'Leary, giving him tuition outside school hours. O'Leary was so impressed with his young pupil that he later recorded that Denis showed a strong determination to master all subjects. By the time he finished his primary education at the age of thirteen, Denis would have been able to read and write both Irish and English. He also would have learned all about the heroes of his native land such as Robert Emmet, Wolfe Tone, Daniel O'Connell and Charles Stewart Parnell, the charismatic leader of the Irish Parliamentary Party whose efforts to secure Irish Home Rule were prominent in the current events at the time. He would also have learned about the 1798 Rebellion and the Fenian uprising, and these episodes would have left an indelible impression on his young mind.

It is not known if Denis was anxious to continue his education after leaving Ballymartle National School, but the reality was that for Denis and the other children of the area a secondary education was practically unavailable. The nearest secondary schools were eleven miles away in Cork city, a huge distance given the lack of transport available. School attendance was not an option unless you were willing to relocate with a relative in the city. For Denis, therefore, the immediate future consisted of remaining at home and helping to work the farm. He maintained his interest in Irish history and continued to read all the books he could on that subject. After eight years working on the farm, however, Denis felt that the time to move on and find employment elsewhere had arrived and in 1903 he left Cullen for Cork where he obtained an apprenticeship with a firm of drapers, O'Sullivan and Howard, at 48–49 Great Georges Street (now Washington Street). This move was to mark the beginning of a new chapter in his life – one that would be dominated by his passion for Gaelic games and athletics, politics and Trade Union affairs.

2

His Sporting Life

From his youth Denis had been an active member of his local GAA club in Ballymartle. After moving to Cork he continued to play hurling with the club which at that time had a good team and which then, as now, were opponents to be respected. His brothers Michael and Batt also played with the club. Other prominent players at the time were the Kellehers of Glinny, the Walshs/Deasys of Riverstick, the Roches, O'Donoghues and Barrys of Cullen, Cronins of Coolcorran and the Colemans of Carhue. Most of these families were in later years to play a major part in the War of Independence.

The regular team during the years 1903–1906 with minor variations was as follows (note that seventeen players turned out on the field of play at that time):

His Sporting Life

M. Roche
D. Barry, D. Coleman, J. Coughlan, D. Kelleher
T. Crowley, J. Deasy, J. Roche
T. Tobin, Fox Walsh
J. Deasy, Con Kelleher, M. Bogue
J. Roche, W. Roche (c), M. Donovan, D. Dennehy

The year 1906 was one of notable achievement. Ballymartle won the Senior Hurling league only to lose the gold medals after an objection to one of their players. They also reached the county senior hurling semi-final only to be beaten by 'The Barrs' (St Finbarr's).

From the *The Blues: A History of St Finbarr's GAA Club* by Seán Beecher we learn of the following:

There is a great deal of confusion regarding the final of the 1905 and 1906 County Championship. It appears that these finals were not played until 1907 and it was agreed that the game between the Barrs and Ballymartle would be for the Championship of both years. The game was played on Feb 4th 1907.

The Venue was Ballinhassig and the crowd was not a great one, the fault being attributed to the railway company's failure to provide a special train for the occasion. Ballymartle surprised the onlookers when they attacked the Barrs and dominated the early part of the game, though not translating their superiority into scores and at half time the Barrs led by 1-5 to 0-4.

The Examiner reported 'Throughout the game, Ballymartle made a distinctly creditable performance, and the form shown by them gave great promise especially when it is considered that they are together only a comparatively short period'.

The final score was St Finbarr's 2-9 Ballymartle 0-6.

The year 1908 saw the club beating Shanbally in Senior and Junior matches played in Ballygarvan. That year also Ballymartle beat the Barrs in the Ballinhassig Senior Tournament, a competition rated next to the County Championship, winning a set of silver medals with gold centres. From 1909 onwards there was no really active team in Ballymartle even though they got together to play matches from time to time.

In 1908 Denis joined the Blackrock Hurling Club and was to play a significant part in a golden era for the club. Denis was a steely tenacious player as a full-back and was known as fair and wiry, someone who showed neither fear nor favour to any opponent. He made his senior debut for the club in 1909.

At that time Blackrock was a small fishing village about 2 miles downstream from Cork city. The well-known landmark, a sixteenth-century castle, is situated a little downriver from the village. Blackrock Hurling Club was established in 1883, one year before the GAA itself was founded. The club was originally known as Cork Nationals until the start of 1888 when it changed its name to the National Hurling Club of Blackrock. Later that year the name was changed again to its present one, Blackrock National Hurling Club. The club colours are a hooped green and orange jersey, which has been worn with pride by some of the greatest hurlers of all time. The club commands great loyalty among its supporters and is affectionately known as 'The Rockies', which was the title of a book published by the club in 1983 to commemorate the centenary of its founding. Denis played with his first winning Blackrock side against Dungourney on 8 August 1910. The result was Blackrock 6-3 Dungourney 3-1.

A German training fleet had arrived in the Port of Cork on the Friday before the game. Seeing the chance to display the national game to distinguished foreigners, J. J. Walsh, President of the County Board, invited 2,000 officers, cadets and sailors to see the County Final. Strictly on time on the Sunday, scores of pinnaces sped up the River Lee and the seamen disembarked near the Athletic Grounds on the Marina. Two thousand seats in a 'privileged' position were reserved for the Germans who, it is reported, enjoyed the game immensely. Needless to mention, the British were irritated at this invitation, as they and the Germans were on very bad terms politically at the time.

After the match, when the Germans were embarking to leave near the present Lee Rowing Club, a local youngster fell into the Lee and was being swept downstream. Two Germans dived into the river and rescued the boy from drowning. Their bravery was later acknowledged when they were decorated by the Kaiser.

An interesting sequel to this story happened in the 1930s when J. J. Walsh and his wife were passengers on the German airship *Hindenburg* flying over South America. The captain of the airship told Walsh that he was the first Irishman to fly on the *Hindenburg*. He also recalled a visit he had made to Cork some years earlier

The Unknown Commandant

and how he had been decorated by the Kaiser for saving a young boy's life. When J. J. told him of his involvement in the episode the German captain was amazed and the Walsh couple enjoyed special guest status for the rest of the journey. Some years later the *Hindenburg* caught fire and was destroyed within one minute while attempting to dock with its mooring mast in New Jersey. J. J. Walsh was later very much involved in the War of Independence. He was to be the first Irishman deported when the First World War began. He was Sinn Féin TD for Cork and from 1918 was banned from setting foot in his native county by the British until the truce in 1921. He subsequently became a Government Minister and a very successful businessman.

From 1900 to 1919 Blackrock played in nine county hurling championship finals. They won six, and that six included the first four-in-a-row from 1910 to 1913. Denis Barry was selected to play in all those teams. It could have been five-in-a-row but for a mix-up at administration level. In the 1914 final against Midleton the match was arranged to be played in Mallow, but on the day, rain fell in torrents. Due to a breakdown in communications Blackrock were under the impression that the match had been postponed and so did not travel to Mallow. However the Midleton team did and the game was awarded to them. To make matters worse 'The Rockies' had been odds-on favourites to win the senior hurling championship that year.

Other great players of those days with Blackrock were Stephen (Steva) Riordan, 'Doorie' Buckley and his brother Gregory, Tom (Parson) Coughlan and his

J. J. Walsh, *First Chairman Cork Brigade of Irish Volunteers*
'History, after all, is in the main the sum total of individual effort,
provided of course, that men are working in unity under the inspiration
of some common cause. I did my humble best and I came into contact
with so many others working likewise to make the harvest . . . One day
men will be gathering even the slightest memories of those years.' J. J.
Walsh – from his book Recollection of a Rebel (*Courtesy of
Blackrock Hurling Club*)

brother Dan, Barry Murphy, Larry Flaherty, Dinny Kidney, Jerh. Deasy, William (Billy) Mackessy, 'Bill Bill' Dorney, his brother (affectionately called 'Down Down'), Walter Parfrey, Tommy Riordan, Paddy ('Carbery') Mehigan, Paddy O'Brien, Charlie Sullivan, Johnnie Madden, Tom Moroney, whose son, also Tom, was much later a well-known soccer player of high repute, Mickey Kidney, Tom Cox, Andy Fitzgerald, Cors. Roynane and Moss Buckley. These men brought a new impetus into the game of hurling, raising it to new heights. They bestrode the playing fields, giants of skill and dedication. Their names will never be forgotten.

On 8 August 1910 Denis won his first Senior Championship Medal with Blackrock. The final score was Blackrock 6-3 Dungourney 3-1.

Denis readily adapted himself to the higher standards of the senior competitions and was soon accepted to rank among the great hurlers of the historic club, which made the famous achievement of winning three more championships in a row, which set a record at that time. The final scores and the finalists were as follows:

1911   Blackrock 3-4 Aghabullogue 0-0
1912   Blackrock 4-2 Redmonds   0-1
1913   Blackrock 3-3 Midleton   2-2

By contributing a major part in these successful results, the calibre of Denis Barry as a first-rate defender was much acclaimed among the top-notch judges of the game. He also played a major part when his club beat Galway in 1911. He was on the Cork team, which won the Munster Senior Hurling Championship. They lost to

Tullaroan Kilkenny in the All-Ireland final by one point. Blackrock defeated the Davis Club of Dublin to win the Croke Cup competition in 1913.

The Blackrock club were always served loyally not only by their players but also by the work of enthusiastic administrators and trainers. Each player was written to on a regular basis, urging him to train and to stay fit for the fray. From 1912 onwards rule changes improved the game. Teams were reduced from seventeen to fifteen players. The outer posts were replaced by a crossbar and the local County Board insisted that all Championship games would be played in the 'Athletic Grounds', now Páirc Uí Chaoimh.

Denis also played Gaelic football and was a defender on the Lees team that won the Junior Championship in 1910. The Lees team represented the drapers' trade assistants employed in city shops. A team called Nils represented the grocery trade. Both of these teams combined with Macroom to win the 1911 title for Cork.

Athletics were very popular in the early decades of the century. They were a means by which participants in Gaelic games could keep fit. It was also part of the weekly Feis, which would be organised in most of the parishes throughout the country. Denis was well known and won many medals for road walking, running and the lift and strike competitions – now known as An Poc Fada. His striking range was between 72 and 78 yards. Denis was the organiser for many of these competitions and he was the Cork representative on the Governing Council of the National Athletic Association. He was also known to be temperate and attentive during his years of employment.

Blackrock National Hurling Club, 1909.

Blackrock Hurling Team 1909. Denis Barry is seated second row on the left. (Courtesy of Blackrock Hurling Club)

24

Blackrock Hurling Champions 1910: Back row (l–r): Wm Parfrey, J. J. Walsh, M. Domey, C. J. Fitzgerald, A. Fitzgerald, J. Deasy, S. Riordan, W. C. Murphy, M. Leahy (Hon Sec), unknown. Middle row (l–r): P. O'Brien, D. Barry, Wm. Mackessy, B. Murphy, Rev. Fr. Sexton, T. Coughlan (Captain). Front row (l–r): D. Kidney, M. Kidney, A. Buckley, C. Royanne, C. O'Sullivan. Denis Barry is second from left in the middle row. (Courtesy of Blackrock Hurling Club)

The Unknown Commandant

Lees Football Team, winners of the Junior Football Championship 1910. Denis Barry is second from left in the back row. This team was nicknamed 'Collars and Cuffs Team' because the players were all employed in the retail trade in the city and generally there would be two or three employees from each of the various shops in the drapery trade. (Barry family archive)

Denis joined the Trade Union movement in 1907 and remained an active member for his lifetime. He became a voluntary trade union official in 1909 in the Irish Drapers' Assistants Benefit and Protective Association. He was actively involved in the issue of Saturday early closing and attended many meetings in the Banba Hall, Dublin, dealing with the matter.

Denis joined the Ancient Order of Hibernians but there are no records to show that he was active in the affairs of that body, which supported John Redmond and the Irish Party. In Cork the Redmondites were opposed by the All for Ireland League under the leadership of William O'Brien. A certificate issued to Denis dated 5 May 1911 shows the Arms of the Four Provinces which are illustrated with the titles in Irish. The figurehead of

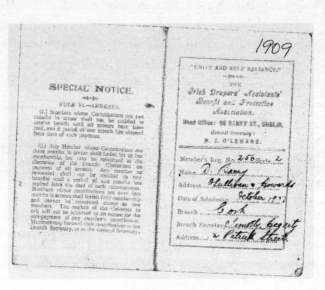

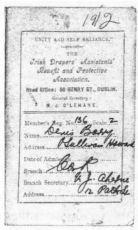

Denis Barry's trade union cards of 1909 and 1912. (Barry family archive)

The Unknown Commandant

Owen Roe O'Neill appears as does the motto of the order displayed in large type: 'Faith and Fatherland'.

Having joined Conradh na Gaeilge Denis attended classes in An Grianán in Queen's Street (now Fr Matthew Street), Cork. It was here that he met kindred spirits who shared his devotion to the study of Irish history, Irish writers and all aspects of national culture. The O'Growney branch of Conradh was formed in Cork in 1907 by Seán O'Hegarty. The study of the writings of P. H. Pearse, *The Singer* and *The Sovereign People*, with lectures from Terence MacSwiney, Tomás MacCurtain and P. S. O'Hegarty (a brother of Seán), were pursued by a very active Craobh of the Conradh.

Denis joined Na Fianna Éireann in 1912, which had a flourishing branch in Cork. He gave both of his energy and his finances to the movement, in as much as his spare time allowed him. His membership of Na Fianna was a major step and on 23 June 1914 Denis enrolled in the Irish Volunteers – Óglaigh na hÉireann. In his signed application he pledged to secure and maintain the rights and liberties common to all the people of Ireland without distinction of creed, class or politics. His enrolment certificate number was 1426, a copy of which is on the facing page. This was now to be Denis' mission in life and he fully understood the commitment and pledged his life to the cause. His brother Michael also joined the movement in the city and his brother Batt joined the Ballinhassig/Ballyheda Company.

Leanfam 50 010c vo clú áp pinnrip.

Company........................ No. 142b

ó5laɪ5 na héɪReann **Irish Volunteers.**

I, the undersigned, desire to be enrolled in the Irish Volunteers, formed

to secure and maintain the rights and liberties common to all the people of

Ireland without distinction of creed, class, or politics

Name........ *Denis Barry* ....

Address........... *25 Barrack St-* ....

Date........... *23/6/14* ....

Corcoran, Printer, 21, Sullivan's Quay, Cork.

A copy of Denis Barry's certificate on joining the Irish Volunteers on 23 June 1914. (Courtesy of Cork City Archives)

3

Politics and Cultural Activities

In April 1915 Denis resigned from his post in O'Sullivan Howard & Co. to take up a more lucrative position with Duggan's 'The Monster House', general drapers in Kilkenny, and on leaving his employers in Cork received the following reference:

> Mr. Denis Barry has been in our employment for twelve years during which time we found him thoroughly honest, strictly temperate and most attentive to business. He now leaves of his own accord. He has a through knowledge of the hosiery, shirt and readymade clothing department.
>
> O'Sullivan, Howard & Co.

Denis soon became one of the chief organisers of the Irish Volunteers in that city and so inevitably came to the attention of the ever vigilant Royal Irish Constabulary. He was being closely monitored by them and their agents, and before long became a 'marked man'.

On 3 May 1916, while Denis was going about his usual duties, the military surrounded his place of work in great numbers and an armed party entered the shop looking for the 'Sinn Féiner'. He was arrested and taken to Kilkenny Jail. Six days later he and five other comrades were taken to Richmond Barracks in Dublin. He was detained there until 13 May when he and hundreds of prisoners arrested during the crackdown after the Easter Rebellion were shipped by cattle boat to Frongoch internment camp at Bala, North Wales.

In a short note to his brother Batt, Denis described his ordeal on the day of his arrest.

Dear Batt.

I am sure by now that you have really formed a dreadful opinion of this kid due to his lack of news. On the 3rd May 1916 a report has come to the shop of I being down for arrest. I am awfully busy dressing a sale window and take all reports carefully 'as I am already aware of the good news' every one is anxious to know who is the Sinn Féiner here. At about 11.30 AM the street is suddenly alive with soldiers all coming in our direction. The shop is surrounded, all windows are ordered to be closed and an armed guard is all around with instructions to fire on any person seen leaving. Around noon two armed parties of 16 each enter the shop and a Policeman with instructions to find Mr. Barry. I now hear the

The Unknown Commandant

managers call Mr. Barry, you are wanted. I walk into the shop to be at once surrounded by soldiers with fixed bayonets and the policeman gives an order 'get your hat and coat'. I am now for the first time a prisoner marched to Kilkenny gaol with a royal guard of 250 infantry and 30 police'.

To understand the context of his arrest, the death of Jeremiah O'Donovan Rossa had taken place in August 1915 and the graveside oration by Patrick Pearse in front of a huge gathering of supporters at the grave of O'Donovan Rossa was the spark that ignited the spirit and militant nature of Irish Nationalism, uniting the IRB, the Irish Citizen Army and the Volunteers.

Life springs from death, and from the graves of patriot men and women spring live nations. The defenders of this realm have worked well in secret and in the open. They think that they have pacified Ireland. They think that they have purchased half of us, and intimidated the other half. They think that they have foreseen everything. They think that they have provided against everything; but the fools, the fools, the fools! they have left us our Fenian dead, and while Ireland holds these graves, Ireland unfree shall never be at peace.

This lead inevitably to plans for rebellion and the outcome was the Easter Rising of 1916. However, after many setbacks, including the scuttling off the coast of Kerry of the *Aud*, a German ship carrying guns, and confusion surrounding orders and countermanding of orders, the Rising went ahead in Dublin only while the rest of the country stood down. As a result the Rising was not a success and so, to prevent further bloodshed, Pearse and his comrades surrendered. The Rising itself could be termed a disaster but it turned out, over the next five years, to be the fuse that lit the flame that led to Irish independence.

After the Rising, the British response was severe. Martial law was imposed by the British Military Governor, Major General Sir John Maxwell, the leaders of the Rising were executed – an event which led to a world outcry – and thousands were arrested and detained, many of whom were shipped by cattle boat to jails and internment camps in England and Wales. Those who were arrested were suspected of being intrinsically connected with the movement, which had led to what the British termed 'The Sinn Féin Rebellion'.

On Wednesday 9 May Denis and other prisoners were marched to Kilkenny railway station under heavy military escort, and conveyed by train to Dublin and were then taken to Richmond Barracks. The conditions and treatment of the prisoners is detailed in the following article reprinted from the *Kilkenny People* of 12 May.

Richmond Barracks

Judging by the display of military on Tuesday the 9th of May, one would not be surprised if we were bound for 'somewhere in France' and not until arrival in Dublin did we ascertain it was Richmond. Fortunately not solitary confinement. This time as 25 of our contingent was relegated to a large room, which has 'accommodation for 9 men'. But apparently 'rebels' are not men. The floor for a bed, one horse blanket for covering, tea (resembling bog water) and dog biscuits for breakfast, bully beef and a second helping of dog biscuit for dinner, a liquid which was neither tea or coffee, nor cocoa for supper, with a superb display of military drilling of recruits, conveying to and fro of prisoners for trial, visiting notables, etc. thrown in as attractions. The sanitary arrangements were not quite as bad as Kilkenny gaol but were certainly defective. As a rule the captains and those in high command were civil. Thus passed the 10th, 11th and 12th of May, and the unlucky 13th dawned dark and foreboding. It seemed as if in the evening of this Saturday that we were to be granted the 'privilege' of a trial judging by the court command of an officer to hand in the names of our Solicitors. But the hope was short lived as a countermanding orders 'prepare to get on the Barrack Square in ten minutes' followed a short time afterwards. For what or for where? 'You aren't to reason why'. Between 500 or 600 lined up and speculation ran high as to our destination. Some said France, some Dartmoor, while others clung to the belief that we would never leave 'the old sod' and inclined to Athlone as the likely destination. The answer from an officer was a look that threatened insult, and as the church bells rung out the evening hour on that dreary cold wet evening, with bare heads and surrounded by bayonets, the Angelus was recited under conditions which are seldom witnessed and rarely experienced. The order 'Quick March' came a few minutes afterwards, and the march was certainly imposing as far as militarism was concerned. En route for the North Wall everything possible was done to prevent an ovation, or even a good bye. Hand waves from windows was suppressed by threatening to shoot, but the old Dublin spirit is not so easily put down and one heard despite military threats and especially below O'Connell street the cries of young and old 'Keep up your hearts, boys!'

Deportation

A cattle boat awaited our arrival at the North Wall and now Irishmen were forced to occupy the places of oxen, but despite all this the characteristics of the Celt were never more manifest. There in that cattle-hold, with the usual display of bayonets overheard, all joined in 'Come Back to Erin' and ere the moorings were cast off the congested 'rebels' to a man went on to their knees and recited the Rosary, first in Irish, then in English, in which was poured forth all the sorrow, tribulation and hope of the Catholic Celt. No force of arms suppressed the 'songs of our own native land' and for five hours speeches, songs and recitations were given without interruption. The Defence of the Realm Act, so far as the boat was concerned was for the time being repealed. Holyhead was reached; a special train awaited our arrival, a fresh escort of military: a nine-hour journey to where nobody knew. Then Wakefield, a short march and jail again. With the memories of Kilkenny prison still fresh in our minds, solitary confinement afforded very little relief. The cell of the same dimensions, the same bare walls, a still larger display of military; the clanging of keys, the slamming of cell doors and once more alone, alone and alone! A half hours exercise was allowed the 'rebels' for the first ten days. This meant 23.5 hours in your cell. Any attempt at speaking, or even attempting to get the benefit of the little air through the ventilator in you cell window, was punishable by 24 hours on bread and water in a 'punishment cell'. The food was poor and scanty, no reading matter was afforded, writing was prohibited and resort to the lavatory in the evenings forbidden. Thus one existed for ten days, when the conditions became a little better, but at no time during our incarceration did the treatment come up to, or even approach, the standard afforded to any criminal who is 'doing time' for any crime no matter how heinous.

The release came like our arrest. It might have meant going on 'bread and water' for all we knew. No charge, no acquittal, no apology; only eight out of twelve released with the writer; only got portion of the cash they deposited on confinement and all articles such as pipes, tobacco, cigarettes, pouches, correspondence and other personal belongings were confiscated. You then got a pass for your destination and were let loose in a strange city. Such were the arrests, such the punishment, and such the release.

In June 1916 Denis Barry, William Denn and John Gibbons were transferred from Wakefield Prison to

Politics and Cultural Activities

Frongoch Internment Camp where they were detained without trial until their release on 24 July 1916.

Tensions at many levels in the country were at an all-time high as this exchange of letters between General Maxwell and the Bishop of Limerick during May 1916 illustrates. The letters were published in the *Kilkenny People*, 3 June 1916.

'Heading Censored'

The following correspondence has taken place between General Maxwell, Commander-in-Chief of the forces in Ireland and most Rev Dr O'Dwyer. Bishop of Limerick.

Headquarters,
Irish Command,
Parkgate,
Dublin

6th May 1916.

My Lord, – I have the honour to request your Lordship's co-operation in a matter connected with the present deplorable situation in Ireland, the settlement of which I am confident you desire no less keenly than I do. There are two priests in your diocese, the Rev Fr _____, of _____Co Limerick and the Rev. Father _____, of _____, Co Limerick, whose presence in that neighbourhood I consider to be a dangerous menace to the peace and safety of the realm, and had these priests been laymen they would have already been placed under arrest. In this case I would be glad if your Lordship will deny their having intercourse with the people, and inform me of your decision – I have the honour to be your obedient servant.

> J G Maxwell
> General Commander-in-Chief
> H M Forces in Ireland

The Most Rev Dr O'Dwyer, Bishop of Limerick
Abbey View,
Kilmallock

9th May 1916

Sir – I am directed by the Bishop of Limerick to acknowledge the receipt on this morning of your letter of the 6th inst, which has been forwarded to him at the above address. The Bishop desires to point out that the action which you suggest to him to take towards Rev Father _____, and the Rev Father _____, would be a very severe punishment, which the Bishop has no right to inflict on these priests except on a definite charge supported by evidence. If then you are good enough to specify the grounds, in which you consider that their presence in the neighbourhood of _____, and _____, is a dangerous menace to the peace and safety of the realm, the Bishop will investigate the matter and inform you his decision. But whatever may be the rights of the military authorities in the exercise under martial law, a Bishop in the exercise of his authority has to follow the rules of ecclesiastical procedure. – I have the honour to be your obedient Servant

James Conor O'Shea
Pro-Secretariat

Headquarters Irish Command
Parkgate Dublin

12th May 1916

My Dear Lord Bishop –
I beg to acknowledge the letter of 9th May from your Lordship's secretary. Father _____ has been reported as on 14th November 1915 speaking in his church at _____ , against conscription is said to have attended a lecture by PH Pearse on the 'Irish Volunteers of '12 and of blessing the colours of the Irish Volunteers at _____, on 2nd January 1916 also speaking at a meeting which took place at _____ on 17th March 1916. Father _____ is said to have been active with a certain E Blythe organising Irish Volunteers. In November 1915 he got printed a large number of leaflets appealing to young men of the Gaelic Athletic Association to join the Irish Volunteers. He is said to be president to the Irish Volunteers at _____ and _____. He is said to have been present at the Irish Volunteers meeting at _____ when a certain John McDermott delivered

inflammatory and seditious speeches on 17th March 1916. When I wrote to your Lordship on the 6th, I hoped that you would have been able to take steps to prevent priests from mixing up in organisations that are a danger to the realm. If these reports be true it should not be necessary for me to make definite charges, supported by evidence against these priests, who, I imagine, will not deny their particulars in the Irish Volunteer Movement, which has led to such deplorable events all over Ireland. Therefore, it should not be difficult for your Lordship, under such disciplinary power as you possess, to prevent at any rate priests from mixing up with and inciting their flock to joining an organisation such as the Irish Volunteers have proved themselves to be – I beg to remain, my dear Lord Bishop, yours very truly,

JG Maxwell

Most Rev. Dr. O'Dwyer, Bishop of Limerick
Ashford, Charleville
17th May 1916

Sir – I beg to acknowledge the receipt of your letter of 12th inst, which has been forwarded to me here. I have read carefully your allegations against Rev _____ , and Rev _____, but do not see in them any justification for disciplinary action on my part. They are both excellent priests, who hold strong National views, but I do not know that they have violated any law, civil or ecclesiastical. In your letter of 6th inst you appealed to me to help you in the furtherance of your work as military dictator of Ireland. Even if action of that kind was not outside my province, the events of the past few weeks would make it impossible for me to have any part in proceedings which I regard as wantonly cruel and oppressive. You remember the Jameson Raid, when a number of buccaneers invaded a friendly State, and fought the forces of the lawful Government. If ever men deserved the supreme punishment it was they. But, officially and unofficially, the influence of the British Government was used to save them, and it succeeded. You took care that no plea for mercy should interpose on behalf of the poor young fellows who surrendered to you in Dublin. The first information which we got of their fate was the announcement they had been shot in cold blood. Personally, I regard your action with horror, and I believe that it has outraged the conscience of the country. Then the deporting by hundreds and even thousands of poor fellows without trial of any kind, seems to me an abuse of power, as fatuous as it is arbitrary, and altogether your regime has been one of the worst and blackest chapters in the history of the misgovernment of this country.

– I have the honour to be, sir your obedient servant,

Edward Thomas O'Dwyer
Bishop of Limerick

Meanwhile the citizens of Kilkenny united and a Wives

and Family Fund was set up by a select committee. This committee made an appeal to the people for financial support for the wives and families of the arrested and detained men. Despite the existence of martial law the local newspaper, the *Kilkenny People*, published the appeal for funds and a strong editorial on 20 May 1916 as follows:

The Voice of the People

Kilkenny appears to us to have been selected for an extra special dose of martial law. The 'mailed fist' and the cold steel storm seem to have been more strongly in evidence here than in any other part of Ireland outside the actual scenes of disturbance. What have we done to deserve all this? Is it that we have been too quiet? Shall we say too meek and subservient? Perhaps, 'the powers that be' considered that 'like a dog and a greenwood tree, the more they bend us the better we'll be'.

We have carefully read the newspapers, in fact, since Easter Monday we have done little else than read newspapers – when we could get them – and we are convinced that Kilkenny was specially victimised. Let us take two Southern cities and a Southern town – Cork, Limerick, and Tralee – each supposed to be a hotbed of Sinn Féinism and each having displayed premonitory symptoms of unrest as evidenced by several prosecutions under the Defence of the Realm Act (we have not had, we believe, a single prosecution under this Act in Kilkenny City and County since the war began, and the Judges of

Politics and Cultural Activities

Assize in their references to us have been as plausible and as courteous as if they were so many Lord Chesterfields). There have been, no doubt, some arrests in the three places mentioned, but proportionately they were not nearly as numerous as in Kilkenny and let this be noted – the arrests were not made until the time fixed by General Maxwell's Proclamation for the surrender of arms had expired.

This drew a sharp response from General Maxwell. He wrote to the editor and managing director of the paper as follows:

Headquarters Irish Command,
Parkgate, Dublin

28th May 1916.

Sir,
My attention has been called to an article appearing in the issue of the Kilkenny People, dated 20th May 1916 entitled 'The Voice of the People'. Portions of that article seem to have been written with the intention of inciting the people against the military authorities.

I have no wish or intention to interface unduly with the liberty of the Press, but inflammatory articles or reports of inflammatory speeches cannot be permitted, and offenders render themselves liable to prosecution, under the Defence of the Realm Act, and possibly to the seizure and destruction of their Press.

The Unknown Commandant

You will therefore, until further orders, submit proofs of the Kilkenny People to the Country Inspector of the Royal Irish Constabulary at Kilkenny, before publication.

> I am, Sir,
> Your Obedient Servant
>
> J. G. Maxwell,
> General Commanding in Chief,
> H.M. Forces in Ireland.

The fund-raising committee continued its work, meeting every Wednesday evening, and recording all donations to the fund. The list of the donors and the amounts contributed were published weekly in the *Kilkenny People*. This committee also received an update on the status of the prisoners. The meeting held on 26 July was informed that all the Kilkenny prisoners with the exception of Peter de Loughry TC (Town Councillor) were now freed. Mr de Loughry was still held in Reading Detention Prison, where his fellow prisoners included Arthur Griffith, Darrell Figgis and J. McBride (brother of Major McBride, executed for his part in the rebellion). It was decided at this meeting to hold a general meeting of subscribers to the fund on Sunday 6 August at three o'clock for the purpose of receiving a full report and a balance sheet, and to decide how do dispose of any surplus funds as remained.

The Kilkenny Wives and Families Fund collected or received a total of £424, which in current values would equate to almost €35,000. This reflects the generosity of

****
* **KILKENNY PEOPLE** *
* CIRCULATES IN THE COUNTIES OF *
* KILKENNY, CARLOW, TIPPERARY, *
* QUEEN'S, WATERFORD & WEXFORD. *
****

The Voice of the People.

(PASSED BY CENSOR).

THE KILKENNY PEOPLE is unable to pub
lish to-day the usual weekly article in
which it addresses its readers.

If the "Voice of the People" cannot
speak free and untrammelled, it will not
speak in the accents of slavery. The
Military Dictator who rules Ireland has
addressed to us the letter given below.
We have replied to that letter, but militarism, acting through its representative
in Kilkenny, Mr. P C Power, County
Inspector R.I.C., not only refuses to us
the right of stating our defence, but also
refuses us an opportunity of making it
plain why our reply does not appear.

Headquarters, Irish Command,

Parkgate, Dublin,

29th May, 1916.

SIR,

My attention has been called to an
article appearing in the issue of the
KILKENNY PEOPLE, dated 20th May
1916, entitled 'The Voice of the People.'
Portions of that article seem to have
been written with the intention of inciting
the people against the military authorities.

I have no wish or intention to interfere
unduly with the liberty of the Press but
inflammatory articles or reports of inflammatory speeches cannot be permitted,
and offenders render themselves liable to
prosecution under the Defence of the
Realm Act and possibly to the seizure
and destruction of their Press

You will therefore until further orders,
submit proofs of the KILKENNY PEOPLE to
the County Inspector of the Royal Irish
Constabulary at Kilkenny, before publication.

I am, Sir,

Your obedient Servant,

J. G. MAXWELL General
Commanding in Chief
H.M. Forces in Ireland.

E. T Keane Esq.,
Editor and Managing Director,
KILKENNY PEOPLE,
Kilkenny.

Reply to General Maxwell.

SIR,

OUR REPLY TO GENERAL MAX
WELL'S LETTER HAS BEEN CEN-
SORED BY MR. P C. POWER
COUNTY INSPECTOR R.I.C.,
ACTING FOR THE MILITARY
DICTATOR.

THE CORRESPONDENCE ARIS
ING OUT OF THE PROHIBITION
BY MR POWER HAS ALSO BEEN
CENSORED

I am, Sir,

Your obedient Servant,

E. T. KEANE,

Managing Director,
KILKENNY PEOPLE LTD.

The response of the Kilkenny People *to Maxwell's demand is shown
above. The image has been reduced for the sake of illustration but one
has to imagine four blank columns on a full broadsheet newspaper page
between the first and second columns as shown. (Courtesy of the*
Kilkenny People)

the *Kilkenny People*, even though some of the people who contributed to the fund were totally opposed to the Easter Rising. Less than £2 of the money collected was spent on the printing of posters and postage.

Two pieces published by the *Kilkenny People* in August 1916 are of particular interest. The item of 5 August 1916 is a statement from the internees detained without charge or trial at Frongoch in North Wales. The statement was from all the internees detained there which would have included those deported after the Easter Rising in Dublin and the men from Kilkenny and other parts of Ireland. The editorial outlines the tactics of the forces of the Crown in and around Kilkenny where they intimidated and terrorised the people. The item of 12 August 1916 sets out in detail the work of the committee, which raised funds for the internees and their families.

5 August 1916
Frongoch Prisoners of War
About two or three weeks ago while the fate of the Lloyd George proposal was still undecided, the Irishmen interned at Frongoch passed the following resolution which was recently handed to us:-

'On behalf of the Irish Prisoners of War interned at Frongoch Internment Camp, fearing lest we might be used as a pawn by the Party Politicians in their bargaining over the partition of the country, desire to make our position clear to our countrymen and women, that we are utterly opposed to such dismemberment on any conditions whatsoever, and repudiate those who desire to make our release from intern-ment an inducement to our people to agree to such proposals.

The Voice of the People

With the release of Mr. Peter de Loughry, T.C. the last of the Kilkenny Martial Law prisoners (with the exception of Captain J. J. O'Connell, who, although not a resident of Kilkenny, was taken into custody in this city, and is still detained) has been set free. The 'rounding up' process, as it was picturesquely described in the sanctimonious British Press, as if the couple of thousand of Irish citizens who were dragged from their homes and their families without warning and without charge were so many wild beasts, began in the case of Kilkenny on Wednesday, April 27, and was continued for the three or four succeeding days. It was carried out by an imposing force – imposing in its numbers though not in its members – of British military, horse, foot and artillery, armoured motor-cars, machine guns, stretcher-bearers, sappers and all the paraphernalia of war. This peaceable and law-abiding city, where every man was free to hold and give expression to his own opinions, political or religious without molestation or insult, was invaded as if by a conquering army; for part of several days cordons of military with fixed bayonets held the street, traffic was suspended, houses were entered, floors torn up, gardens dug up and from the roof of a Cinema Hall, reputed to be a veritable arsenal, the eagle-eyed County Inspector, vigilant watchdog of the Empire, with beetled brow and Napoleonic pose, discerned a burning furze bush to which an innocent and hard-working peasant, fresh from the perusal of the latest leaflet from the Department of Agriculture, had just applied a match on the slopes of Mount Leinster and being, like a poet, 'of imagination all compact' he interpreted it – not according to the Mosaic Law, but according to the Dublin Castle code, which is certainly far removed from all religious sanction – as a pre-arranged signal portending grave danger to the stability of those institutions which, amongst other good things, provide a career open to such talent as is possessed by gentlemen such as he and those who aided and abetted him in the carrying out of the Easter manoeuvres in this peaceable city.

The search for arms, zealously, if not over-zealously, conducted, proved a futile and fruitless labour; and the only incriminating piece of evidence found – apart from the burning bush which set fire to the County Inspector's imagination – was contained in a few lines taken from the following verse of a poem know to every schoolboy, which were displayed in the Assembly Hall of the Kilkenny Volunteers.

Let cowards sneer and tyrants frown,
Oh little do we care!
A felon's cap the noblest crown
An Irish head can wear
And every Gael in Innisfail,
Who scorns the serf's vile brand.
From Lee to Boyne will gladly join
The felons of our land.

Politics and Cultural Activities

The military destroyed the sheet of paper on which these words were inscribed. Wherever they have succeeded in destroying the sentiment that inspires and underlies the words – wherever, in fact, they or those who set them to work have not succeeded in reviving and intensifying that sentiment – is a matter on which thoughtful and unprejudiced mind may not unprofitably ponder.

All the men who were arrested during the White Terror that reigned for a week in Kilkenny have now been restored to their homes – no, not all! One of them was summoned before the Supreme Court-Martial, securely guarded though he was by guns and bayonets. So let us concede that martial law is entitled to claim one victim in Kilkenny.

12 August 1916
'I desire to thank most sincerely the men who were associated with me in the work of raising and distributing the fund. In particular I would like to mention the invaluable services rendered by Mr. Dan O'Connell, who indeed, far more than myself, discharged the duties of secretary and treasurer to the Committee, and who has worked unsparingly and unselfishly to carry out the object for which the fund was subscribed. I would also like to make special mention to the great trouble taken by Mr. P. Corcoran, who has personally visited the families of the prisoners and distributed the grants made by this Committee, and to whom the Committee, and the Nationalists of the city and county are under a deep debt of gratitude.

The Unknown Commandant

In addition to the cases of Kilkenny prisoners, two other cases came under the consideration of the Committee and grants were made in respect thereof. One was the case of a young Kilkenny man who was arrested for his part in the Rebellion at Enniscorthy and to whose dependents, residing in Johnstown in this country, weekly grants were made since the case was brought under the notice of the committee after Mr. Drew's balance sheet was prepared, and a grant was voted at the last meeting. Both these young Irishmen, I am glad to say, have now also been released.

'In addition to the grants directed to the families of the prisoners, money was also voted for the purpose of providing food for the prisoners themselves while detained in Wakefield Prison. This money was distributed with the greatest care and economy by two very noble Irish nuns, one of them a Kilkenny lady, who were in constant communication with the Committee and upon whose advice and suggestion the Committee acted.

'In conclusion, I desire to say that, to the best of their ability the Committee carried out the intention of the subscribers and I think it is desirable to mention that the entire expenses incurred in the raising of this very large sum of money – namely £424 9s 8d – only amounted to £1 2s 8d, of which sum 12s 6d was the printing of circulars and the balances for postage. I think this constitutes a record, which has not been equalled.'

Politics and Cultural Activities

In August 1916 Denis Barry returned to his job in Kilkenny following his stay in Frongoch and after a short break resumed his political activities and his duties in the Kilkenny City Brigade. The Irish people were now fully energised and were more determined than ever to rid the country of the occupier. Denis played a major part in the successful election campaign of William T. Cosgrave in a by-election for Kilkenny held in August 1917. This was a further success for the Sinn Féin/Volunteer movement following the victory of de Valera in the East Clare constituency in July. The Volunteers were by that time appearing openly as a fully disciplined force, wearing uniforms, when acting as election workers. Election fervour in those days was high but the Volunteers maintained order even though they used sticks and hurleys and did not yet display guns in public.

At the Sinn Féin Árd Fheis held in 1917 all the parties that opposed British Rule in Ireland agreed on a common policy, namely, to work for the establishment of an Irish Republic. Sinn Féin promised that its elected members would not take their seats in the British Parliament.

Sinn Féin committed to forming its own government (Dáil Éireann) in the forthcoming general election to be held in November 1918. They also vowed to undermine British rule in Ireland. The result of the 1918 general election showed that Sinn Féin candidates won 73 seats and were elected to the new Dáil Éireann.

4

Struggle for Independence

In November 1918 when Denis Barry returned to Cork he was appointed to the Brigade Staff of the Cork No. 1 Brigade. He was designated as an intelligence officer reporting to Tomás MacCurtain and Terence MacSwiney. He set up his own business as a wholesale agency in gents clothing. This business did not conflict in any way with his duties and obligations to the Republican movement.

Dáil Éireann was for the first time elected in 1918 and met in the Mansion House in Dublin in January 1919, even though a considerable number of elected members were still imprisoned by the British. Cathal Brugha was appointed President of the Ministry. He nominated the following ministries:

Struggle for Independence

Finance	E. MacNeill
Foreign Affairs	Count Plunkett
Home Affairs	M. Collins
National Defence	R. Mulcahy
Speaker of the House	Seán T. O'Kelly

Cathal Brugha selected Conor Maguire, a young Mayo solicitor who was active in Sinn Féin, to help draft the judicial rules for the newly established Republican Courts. Maguire also served as a land judge in the legal system that emerged during the War of Independence. He was later to represent the Barry family in a case before the Master of the Rolls after the Free State Government refused to hand over the mortal remains after Denis Barry's death. Maguire made an important contribution to the Irish legal system, and was Attorney General in the first Fianna Fáil administration. He was President of the High Court in 1936 and became Chief Justice in 1946. He was elected Uachtarán of Oireachtas na Gaelige in 1962.

Denis as a member of the Brigade Staff was appointed head of the Irish Republican Police (IRP) in the Cork Brigade area. This force, which was an unarmed one, was set up by Dáil Éireann. The RIC (Royal Irish Constabulary) had at this stage been driven from their stations and barracks, particularly in rural areas. The Volunteer officers felt that the huge increase in lawlessness needed to be addressed and courts were set up in well-known safe locations where an appointed judge would preside. Volunteers would act as police to carry out judgements of the Court. The types of offences dealt with by the courts were 'rowdyism', larceny, breaches of the licensing laws, damage to property, bank and post office robberies and assaults. Punishments for these offences varied and included returning any stolen property, making restitution or repairing damage. Fines were also imposed. Denis and the Volunteers working under him ensured that court orders were enforced.

Since the IRP had no jails to confine offenders, a partial solution was found in that some of those convicted by the courts were exiled to small and unpopulated islands off the south and west coasts of Ireland. In one reported incident, three offenders who had been banished by a Republican Land Court to an island for three weeks refused to be rescued by the RIC declaring that since they were citizens of the Irish Republic the RIC had no authority over them.

The IRP had a strong presence in twenty-one of Ireland's thirty-two counties and the *Irish Bulletin*, the official Dáil newspaper, claimed that they had arrested eighty-four criminals in twenty-four counties within two weeks. The IRP recruits generally came from the Irish Republican Army. In the city of Cork, where the IRP had a considerable presence, the IRA elected officers for duty with the police force. They operated according to IRA Brigade structures and each unit was headed by a brigade staff officer. Denis was the Cork No. 1 Brigade officer. They did not wear a uniform; however, in the Cork area most of the units had armbands with the letters 'IRP' displayed. It was the first unarmed police force operating with the authority of Dáil Éireann.

Denis Barry's efforts to make Cork safe was well appreciated by those in authority at that time. In tributes made after Denis' death, the then Bishop of Cork, Daniel Cohalan, wrote that he knew Denis, and knew him to be a very good man. Mr G. Nason, President of the Cork Workers Council, referred to Denis as a worker and also a man who endeared himself to a good many people of the city, especially during the Black and Tan times when he filled the position of Chief Commissioner of Police in Cork. Members of the Council met him on many occasions on labour questions and also on charitable matters and he never showed the cold shoulder to them. Councillor Hennessy of the Cork Corporation stated that he knew Denis for many years and that for up to twelve years he had rendered services to his country in every way without ever expecting to be rewarded. During the troubled times he could testify to the fact that Denis never went to bed until three or four o'clock in the morning because his duty compelled him to walk the streets and keep the city free from crime.

In late 1919 and the early months of 1920 the IRA was reorganised along different lines. In each Brigade area flying columns of 100 to 150 Volunteers became full-time soldiers who, after intensive training, moved and attacked over a wide area. They hit hard and withdrew speedily, inflicting heavy causalities on the army of occupation. Small units, known as Active Service Units (ASUs) were now fully trained and operated in the cities.

In Cork city Tomás MacCurtain was elected by the Corporation as the first Republican Lord Mayor of the city. Volunteers were now appearing in public in uniform and had the support and help of most of the citizens. However, by mid March after a series of fatal shootings of British forces and the shooting of some exposed spies, a murder most foul was committed. Armed soldiers with blackened faces arrived at Thomas Davis Street to the Blackpool home of the Lord Mayor. Having forced entry into the house, they shot to death Tomás MacCurtain while his wife, Eilís, and young children looked on. The dead Lord Mayor was attended to by Fr Dominic O'Connor, a well-known Capuchin priest, the local District Nurse Cahill and Flor O'Donoghue (IRA Director of Intelligence), who arrived after being alerted of the event.

The British propaganda machine went into action and they denied that they were responsible. Some of our revisionist historians have claimed that his own had carried out the murder, but a jury verdict recorded that Tomás MacCurtain was murdered by the forces of the British Crown. He was buried after solemn High Mass in the North Cathedral and after a full military funeral was laid to rest in the Republican Plot in St Finbarr's Cemetery in Cork. This plot was reserved by the Cork Corporation for officers, Volunteers and Fianna Éireann who died in the War of Independence and thereafter.

The British response was to organise a militia force, some of whom were drawn from criminal elements stood down after the First World War. They arrived in Ireland, some in uniform and more in khaki pants and dark police jackets. They became known as the Black and Tans because of their appearance, although some local people believe their name came from a pack of hunting hounds also known by that name. They arrived in March 1920. One of their divisional commanders, a Lt. Col. Smyth, was appointed divisional police commissioner for Munster.

The lying-in-state of the murdered Lord Mayor of Cork, Tomás Mac Curtain. The honour guard can be seen wearing military uniform (which was illegal under British rule). (Courtesy of Osprey)

He addressed his police personnel and ordered them as follows:

> If a police Barracks is burned or if the barracks already occupied is not suitable, then the best house in the locality is to be commandeered and the occupants thrown into the gutter. Let them die there – the more the merrier.
>
> Should the order 'Hands Up' not be immediately obeyed, shoot and shoot with effect. The more you

shoot the better I will like you and I assure you no policeman will get into trouble for shooting any man. (*The Burning 1920* by Pearse Lawlor)

On 11 May 1920 a British cabinet meeting, which was also attended by General Nevil Macready (then OC British Forces Ireland), decided to send eight further battalions of regular troops to Ireland. Two days later they announced a new force to be organised to assist the law. They were to be called Auxiliaries to the police and they were mainly ex-army officers who had seen service in the Great War. They became known as '£1 per day all found men' and it was laid down for them that they were not subject to military discipline. At this stage Lloyd George offered General Macready command of all the British forces in Ireland.

Shortly after this the aforementioned Smyth was dining at the Cork County Club on South Mall with Inspector Craig when six Volunteers, commanded by Dan 'Sandow' O'Donovan, entered the club and confronted Smyth and Craig.

'Were not your orders to shoot on sight?' asked Sandow. 'Well, you are in our sights now, so prepare to die.'

The Volunteers opened fire, Smyth was shot dead and Craig slightly injured. A large crowd gathered on the street outside the club. A group of soldiers and Black and Tans arrived and opened fire on the crowd injuring about forty citizens. Major General Strickland issued the following curfew: 'I hereby order and require that any person within a three mile radius of the Post Office, Oliver Plunkett St. remains indoors between the hours of

Struggle for Independence

10 pm and 3 am. Only people with a Military permit are exempt from this order.'

Terence MacSwiney was elected Lord Mayor of Cork after the murder of Tomás MacCurtain. MacSwiney, who was a well-known author and politician, was at the heart of the Irish cultural revival at the beginning of the twentieth century. He was a founder member of the Cork Celtic Literary Society and wrote numerous poems for the Society's Journal. With Daniel Corkery he founded the Cork Dramatic Society and wrote many plays. He also wrote a series of articles for the journal *Irish Freedom* between 1912 and 1916. These articles were published posthumously as *Principles of Freedom* in 1921 in the United States and Ireland.

MacSwiney's love of the Irish language was such that he held classes in An Grianán in Queen Street (now Father Matthew Street) in Cork. His leadership of the Volunteers in Cork was the work of blending all the varying societies together. He can be favourably compared to Patrick Pearse and James Connolly in his vision to see Ireland Gaelic and free. He performed his duties as Lord Mayor and Commandant of Cork No. 1 Brigade very diligently, working long hours.

On the night of 20 August 1920 Terence summoned the members of his Brigade Council to a meeting in the City Hall. A meeting of senior IRB officers was also taking place there and a Republican Court was in session in another part of the building. Commandant Denis Barry was amongst those in the City Hall that night.

Shortly after 7.30 p.m. six armoured cars and almost 300 troops from Victoria Barracks (now Collins Barracks)

The Unknown Commandant

The committee of Cork No. 1 Branch ITGWU 1920 (James Connolly Memorial Branch). Back row (l–r): T. Mulhall, R. O'Keeffe, D. Healy, D. J. Galvin, J. J. Murphy, T. O'Sullivan, Con Murphy, W. Deasy, J. O'Keeffe. Middle row (l–r): T. McCarthy, L. Prior (Assistant Secretary), M. Carey, D. Collins, J. Fitzpatrick, J. Sheehan TC, Thomas Coyle (General Steward), J. Murphy, J. Casey, Denis Barry TC, E. O'Brien, B. Kelleher. Front row (l–r): P. Barry, D. O'Riordan, R. Walsh, S. Heffernan, Ald. Tadhg Barry (Secretary), Joseph O'Keeffe, W. Kenneally (Chairman), Rev. Fr Peter OFM, M. Hill (ex Rep), R. Day TC, D. Buckley, S. O'Connell. (Courtesy of Evening Echo)

stormed the building and detained most of the people on the premises. Eleven men were arrested and taken to the Detention Barracks and all the rest were released by 9.30 p.m. Lord Mayor MacSwiney; Seán Ó Hegarty, Vice O.C Cork No. 1 Brigade; Joe O'Connor, Quartermaster; Dan O'Donovan OC 1st Battalion; Mick Lynch, OC 4th Battalion; Liam Lynch, OC 2nd Cork Brigade; and Pat McCarthy Mick Carey, Tom Mulcahy and Pat Harris were all arrested.

MacSwiney refused to hand over his chain of office but he and his comrades were stripped of all their possessions. They told their captors that they would join their comrades in Cork Jail in a hunger strike, which had been begun on the previous day because of their detention without charge or trial. MacSwiney was known to his captors but the others had given false names and after three days were released without charge.

The events of the night of 12 August suggests that someone had informed the British of the meetings but their intelligence was so bad that they failed to recognise some of the top officers they had captured but released. MacSwiney was court-martialled in Victoria Barracks on 16 August and was found guilty of three of the four charges against him. He defended himself, informing the court that it was a grave offence to commit any act against the elected head of a city and he dismissed the charges laid against him. He concluded by stating that since he had taken no food since Thursday, he would be free in a month, thereby limiting any term of imprisonment the court could impose.

MacSwiney was sentenced to two years and was transferred by boat through South Wales and then on to be incarcerated in Brixton Prison, London. There he began the hunger strike which led to his death.

Donal O'Callaghan was elected deputy Lord Mayor of Cork and Seán O'Hegarty took command of the Cork No. 1 Brigade. The Brigade at this time was volatile and frustrated having lost the murdered Lord Mayor MacCurtain and now Terence MacSwiney from its numbers.

Intelligence given to O'Hegarty suggested that DI Swanzy was the man responsible for the death of MacCurtain. The RIC transferred Swanzy to Lisburn, County Antrim. Contact was made with Michael Collins and Cathal Brugha and they agreed that an operation could take place to shoot Swanzy. Seán Culhane and four Volunteers went to Belfast and linked up with a member of the Belfast Brigade who had carried out surveillance on Swanzy. A revolver used by Tomás MacCurtain was carried by the Cork team. When Swanzy left the cathedral in Lisburn shortly after one o'clock a member of the Cork Brigade, using MacCurtain's gun, shot him dead.

Denis Barry retained his involvement in the Trade Union movement. Having joined the Irish Drapers' Assistants Union in 1907 he was still active in the movement. He was present when Rev. Fr Peter OFM unfurled the new flag of the Irish Transport and General Workers' Union in 1920. This union is now known as SIPTU and celebrated its centenary in 2009. Denis received the following interesting letter from Union H.Q. in Dublin.

30 June 1919
Dear Denis

Re: Saturday early closing

Will you please inform the members of your staff that a meeting with reference to Saturday early closing will be held in the Banba Hall on Thursday next 3rd July at 7.30 pm sharp. As this matter is of great urgency it is imperative that all those affected should be present.
Please give the members in your house notice at once.

The Unknown Commandant

Also please display the enclosed notice in a prominent place.

Faithfully yours
R.N. Lamb
Branch Secretary

The eyes of the world were now focused on London's Brixton Prison where the long agony continued for Terence MacSwiney. His sister, Máire, stated that at least he had a comfortable bed, warm clean clothing, a fire and careful attention, which made the physical suffering easier. He also had the comfort and consolation of relatives constantly with him. Attempts were made in Cork to capture General Strickland to hold him with a view to obtaining the release of MacSwiney. These attempts were to prove unsuccessful.

The hunger strike in Cork Jail continued. On 17 October 1920 Mick Fitzgerald from Fermoy died after fasting for sixty-seven days. He had been arrested and detained without charge or trial. His remains were carried by his comrades to St Peter and Paul Church in the city centre. When the funeral Mass was concluding, a large party of British forces in full battledress invaded the church, some climbing over the seats to reach to sanctuary. An officer with a drawn revolver gave notice to the priest and to all those present that only 100 people would be permitted in the funeral procession. Thousands of people had crowded into Patrick Street at this stage. When the cortège left the church, Fitzgerald's comrades formed a guard of honour and accompanied by the crowd, and troops in armoured cars walked in military formation to the city boundary. From here the hearse containing his coffin and with his comrades using any available transport proceeded to Kilcrumper Cemetery, Fermoy, where Fitzgerald was laid to rest with full military honours. Once more the presence of British at the service did not deter leaders of the Republican Army from being present.

Eight days later Joe Murphy, a Cork Volunteer, died after seventy-six days on hunger strike. Murphy was a loyal and trusted Volunteer. Despite orders from the British, he was buried in the Republican Plot after solemn High Mass in the Church of the Immaculate Conception, The Lough, Cork, with full military honours.

That same day in Brixton Prison Terence MacSwiney died after a 74-day fast. News of his death spread throughout the world and condemnation of the British

(Left) Volunteer Joe Murphy who died on 25 October 1920 and (right) the watch worn by Joe Murphy. (Courtesy of the Delany family)

The Unknown Commandant

A group of prominent Republicans, who travelled from Cork to join the MacSwiney family to bring home the remains of Terence Mac Swiney, seen here in Regent Street, London. Denis Barry is included in this group, tenth from right. (Barry family archive)

was widespread. When his funeral arrangements were announced, thirty of his comrades, including Denis Barry, went to London to attend Mass and to escort his remains home to his native Cork. On 25 October 1920, after an inquest held in London, his remains were taken to St George's Cathedral, Southwark, where a solemn requiem Mass took place on 28 October. His remains were then carried in dignified procession through the streets of London to Euston Station for transfer to the boat train

from Holyhead to Dublin. However, the British refused to allow the coffin bearing his remains to proceed to Dublin, in order to prevent a major show of support in that city and on the route to Cork. The scenes at Holyhead were described in the *Cork Examiner* of 30 October as 'shocking'. The coffin was placed on the *Rathmore* for shipment to Cork. The family and escort travelled by boat to Dublin and by train to Cork. When the *Rathmore* arrived in Queenstown (Cobh) the coffin was transferred to a tugboat. Thousands of people were waiting when the tugboat arrived at Custom House Quay at 4 p.m. A large force of military was in attendance but withdrew to barracks. When the family arrived the coffin was taken from the tugboat and, shouldered by MacSwiney's comrades and flanked by a guard of honour, his remains were carried to Cork City Hall. The coffin was placed toward the top of the main hall and flanked by Volunteers in IRA uniforms. Thousands of people filed past the remains in dignified silence. Representatives from all public bodies, Conradh na Gaeilge, the GAA and other organisations from all over Ireland were present. On Sunday morning the remains were carried in procession to the North Cathedral where the requiem Mass was concelebrated by Archbishop of Cashel and four other bishops including the Bishop of Cork. After the Mass the funeral procession made its way to St Finbarr's Cemetery, Glasheen Road. Following the prayers Terence MacSwiney was buried next to his comrades Tomás MacCurtain and

Members of Cumann na mBan at the funeral of Terence MacSwiney.
(*Courtesy of* Evening Echo)

Struggle for Independence

Joe Murphy. After the oration full military honours were rendered by his fellow officers

Denis played an active part in the rescue of Seán MacSwiney (brother of Terence), Tom Malone and Con Twomey, Republicans imprisoned on Spike Island in County Cork. Word had reached the movement that the British intended to execute some of the prisoners of whom Seán, Tom and Con were believed to be the most likely. Denis, instructed by Brigade HQ, went to Cobh to meet Company Captain Michael Burke. They both returned to Cork where a meeting under the command of Dan 'Sandow' O'Donovan took place in Masters Restaurant in Marlboro Street.

A plan was drawn up and executed as follows: a motor launch from Cobh, ostensibly on a fishing trip, was seized with the connivance of the owner, Master Mariner Ned O'Regan and, with the Union Jack fluttering astern, set off with Michael Burke, George O'Reilly, Frank Barry and Andrew Butterly on board. Denis had arranged for two of the Ballinhassig Company, Seán Hyde and Jerome Crowley, to meet the escapees and their rescuers at 'Paddy Rock' near Ringaskiddy with transport at the ready. The plan was carried out to perfection. The three men were driven off in a horse and trap and were taken care of by the local company. Michael Burke and Andrew Butterly took the train from Monkstown to Cork and reported to the Brigade's 'clearing house', Wallace's Shop in St Augustine Street, returning home afterwards to Cobh. Meanwhile, George O'Reilly and Frank Barry crossed the river on the ferry to Rushbrook and made their way back to Cobh.

The Unknown Commandant

Nora and Sheila Wallace were committed Republicans. Their shop in St Augustine Street was often used by members of Cork No. 1 Brigade for the passing of messages, etc., between the various units. Nora was a fully trusted Communications Officer to the Brigade Staff.

The war continued with the flying columns taking on the British forces in many battles. Ambushes were now a regular occurrence. The Soloheadbeg Ambush, on 21 January 1919, carried out near Tipperary by Dan Breen, Seán Treacy and fellow Volunteers, proved the effectiveness of guerrilla tactics and was to be the forerunner for many more that took place in the Cork area during 1920 and 1921. The Kilmichael Ambush was led by General Tom Barry on 28 November 1920. Seventeen Auxiliaries were killed in this ambush. This event enraged the British and on the night of 11 December they retaliated. In one of the worst atrocities committed during the War of Independence, British forces deliberately set fire to several blocks of buildings along the east and south sides of Patrick Street in Cork during Saturday night and the following Sunday morning.

The arson and looting by these forces commenced at approximately 10.00 p.m. in Grants & Co. Drapery Warehouse. Shortly after midnight Cash and Co. and the Munster Arcade were reported to be on fire. The City Hall, the Carnegie Library and fifteen other business premises were torched. The British military authorities blamed the Volunteers at first, although most of their forces were roaming about the inner city. Records show that the majority of them returned to barracks at 5.00 a.m. and the remainder at around 8.00

Struggle for Independence

A view of Cork City Hall before the burning. In the foreground Parnell Bridge can be seen. This was a swing bridge, which allowed schooners and small craft access to the south channel of the Lee, and was replaced by the present-day Parnell Bridge on 24 May 1971. The hut on the footpath was, in fact, the control room. (Barry family archive)

a.m. on Sunday morning. The few fire engines available were impeded by some of the soldiers, many of whom were drunk on alcohol stolen from looted premises. The citizens of Cork, emerging from their houses on Sunday morning, were shocked and found great difficulty coming to terms with the scale of destruction in the city. The Chief Secretary for Ireland, Sir Hamar Greenwood, immediately denied that Crown forces were responsible for the conflagration. He also refused demands for an impartial enquiry which was called for by several public bodies in Cork. In spite of Greenwood's obstinacy a booklet published by the Irish Labour Party and Trades

The Unknown Commandant

Union Congress appeared in January 1921 entitled *Who Burned Cork City?* which, on the evidence of eyewitnesses to the events, showed that British forces had set fire to large sections of the city. The eyewitness depositions had been gathered by Séamus Fitzgerald and the statements collated by Alfred O'Rahilly, a future president of University College Cork. A British Army enquiry subsequently placed the blame for the fire on renegade members of a company of Auxiliaries.

This devastating event for Cork and its citizens provoked a peculiar response from the then Bishop of Cork, Daniel Cohalan. On Sunday at midday Mass in St Mary's Church – better known in Cork as the North Cathedral – Bishop Cohalan made no reference to the burning of the city. Instead he devoted his sermon to a tirade against the Volunteers. This was the same man who in a letter six weeks earlier to the *Cork Examiner* on the return to Cork of the remains of Terence MacSwiney suggested that he understood the sacrifices of Robert Emmet, Pearse and the other martyrs of Irish freedom. On 15 December he wrote a letter to the same newspaper vilifying the Volunteers about the Kilmichael Ambush and how this had resulted in the murder of a Dunmanway priest, Canon Magner, by British forces. Many letters were passed between various divisions of the British forces and the Bishop, offering sympathy on the death of Canon Magner but not a word was said by either party about the murder of Tadhg Crowley who was shot on the same day by the same man.

A pastoral letter from this bishop, which was to be read in all Catholic churches in his diocese on Sunday

The cleaning-up process in Cork after the 'The Burning of Cork'. (Barry family archive)

19 December 1920, was effectively a decree of excommunication. A short section of this letter reads as follows:

The Unknown Commandant

> Besides the guilt involved in these acts by reason of their opposition to the law of God, anyone who shall, within the diocese of Cork, organise or take part in the ambush or in kidnapping or otherwise shall be guilty of murder or attempt at murder and shall incur by that very fact the censure of excommunication.

Some historians have justified this decree on the basis of his position as Bishop. Assumptions are made that all of the clergy were in agreement with it. Such is not the case. A Farranferris-based priest, Fr Tom Duggan (later Archdeacon), publicly opposed it. Many more priests voiced their opposition to it publicly. Some refused to read the pastoral letter at Mass and invited members of the congregation to go to the sacristy and read it for themselves. The majority of the officers and Volunteers were fully practising Roman Catholics, including Denis Barry who was a daily attendee at Mass where possible: the Volunteers who were on active service always attended to their religious duties. A public response to the decree was issued by Fr Dominic O'Connor, chaplain to Cork No.1 Brigade (quoted in Kevin Girvan's book *Seán O'Hegarty*). In his letter, Fr O'Connor stated:

> Kidnapping, ambushing, killing, ordinarily would be grave sins or violations of church law, and if these acts were being performed by the volunteers as private persons (whether physical or moral) they would fall under the excommunication . . . hence these acts performed by the Irish Volunteers (the army of the Republic) are, not only not sinful, but

are good and meritorious. And therefore, the excommunication does not affect us.

It has never been stated that this decree applied to any Roman Catholics serving with the British Army, Auxiliaries or the Black and Tans in the Bishop's diocese.

Denis Barry and his team were on duty on that night when Cork city centre and the City Hall were set alight by the British. They arrested a large number of citizens who were looting property and generally taking advantage of a very serious situation. Most of the recovered stolen property was returned by Denis and his men to the rightful owners. Shortly after the event Denis personally returned silver and other religious items to Egans of Patrick Street to the value of more than £9,000 – almost €500,000 in current values. The consequences of this latter action by Denis may have influenced certain ecclesiastical decisions taken following his death (see chapter 5).

On that night also, the two Delany brothers were shot in their beds. Jeremiah died immediately and his brother, Cornelius, died six days later. Both were active members of the First Battalion of the Cork No. 1 Brigade. Their murders were a serious loss to the Volunteer movement. Both are buried in the Republican Plot in St Finbarr's cemetery.

General Strickland ordered the 'K' Company of the Auxiliaries to redeploy from Victoria Barracks to Dunmanway on 13 December. This Company was widely believed to have had a major part in the burning of Cork and the decision was seen by many as a disciplinary one taken to placate Strickland's political masters.

The Unknown Commandant

IRA ambushes on British military forces continued, the most notable being at Coolavokig on 25 February 1921, Clonbanin on 3 March 1921 and at Crossbarry on 19 March 1921. There were many more, especially in the counties of Cork and Kerry.

The British were now claiming success with the discovery of weapons and safe houses for men on the run. The activities of the so-called Anti-Sinn Féin Society were suspected of leading to the arrest of IRA members. The Cork city IRA forces assassinated seven men and wounded another. A ninth man, who was a suspected spy, committed suicide. The IRA also killed four military intelligence officers and four civilians accused of spying. The war was now at stalemate. Both sides were doubtful if a military victory could be achieved by either side.

Troops leaving Victoria Barracks (now Collins Barracks), Cork. (Courtesy of Osprey)

Struggle for Independence

Michael Collins felt that it could last only three to four weeks but men like Tom Barry and Seán Moylan and the Brigade staff felt that they could carry on for many more years. However, tentative soundings revealed that maybe the time had come for talks. Between June and July a series of meetings between the warring sides took place. A truce was agreed and from 11 July 1921 no officially sanctioned actions were to take place.

Each branch of Sinn Féin held meetings to discuss the proposed Treaty. Delegates selected at these meetings were mandated as to which way they were to vote. These meetings also instructed the TDs to vote against the document.

A letter sent to Séamus MacGearailt, Sinn Féin TD for East Cork, by Seán Ó Mórdha, Rúnaí of Comhairle Cheanntair, Cathrach Corcaighe. (Barry family archive)

Seán Ó Mórdha was born in November 1894. He taught in the North Monastery School, Cork. He joined the Sinn Féin movement and was later appointed as Rúnaí of Comhairle Cheanntair, Cathrach Corcaighe. He became a member of the Cork City Library Committee in 1935 and was elected Chairman of that Committee in 1939. He retained that position until his untimely death in 1951. His sister, Mary Ellen Hegarty (née Moore), was an active member of Cumann na mBan. (Barry family archive)

5

Civil War and Tragedy

During the truce Denis Barry was actively engaged in visiting the Brigade Company areas and tightening the discipline of the Republican Police there. The effectiveness of his supervision was reflected in the way in which crimes were detected and the incidence of larcenies reduced. He retained the loyal support of all under his command and the full co-operation of the officers and volunteers generally so that Cork city and its environs became known for the law-abiding conduct of its citizens.

When the Treaty was signed, Denis, with the vast majority of the Cork No.1 Brigade, refused to accept it and it was with a saddened heart that he lived through the months of division and disillusionment among the comrades who had previously fought together against the common enemy with heroic courage and pure-souled idealism. He remained steadfastly at his post as Chief Police Officer until his area was occupied by the Free State forces. For a period he served with the Brigade Active Service Unit until he was appointed to fill the vacancy of Southern Brigade Intelligence Officer. His task in that force was made doubly difficult because of the many arrests of Battalion Intelligence Officers and the animosity of the pro-treaty members of the population.

When the Treaty was agreed between the British and Irish delegations and the Irish delegates presented it to Dáil Éireann, it became clear that a major split was going to happen. The debate that ensued was carried on with much bitterness, some political but mostly personal. A lot of intimidation of members of the Dáil took place, with death threats and the various factions instructing their representatives how to vote. Finally the Treaty was approved by sixty-four votes to fifty-seven. Of the thirty-one TDs who were interned in Frongoch in 1916–1917, fifteen voted for and fifteen voted against the Treaty. Deputy Frank Drohan from Waterford, who was mandated by his Comhairle Ceanntair to vote for the Treaty, resigned his position. The capture at sea of a British Admiralty vessel secured arms for the anti-treaty side. J. J. Walsh, who was one of the founding members of the Irish Volunteers in Cork, voted for the Treaty.

On 9 April 1922, the IRA repudiated the authority of the Dáil, and set up its own Army Council with General Liam Lynch as its Chief of Staff. Four days later, they took possession of the Four Courts in Dublin. The handing over, on 18 May, of Victoria Barracks in Cork by Captain Hugo MacNeill on behalf of the provisional government to Seán O'Hegarty OC, Cork No. 1 Brigade, was a contentious issue and in early June 1922 O'Hegarty resigned from the Army Executive of the IRA over the issue of the pending Civil War.

A general election was held on 16 June 1922 and, during the counting of votes in the constituency of North, Mid, and South, and Southeast Cork, a problem arose in which Denis Barry had a role in resolving. It also indicates that the hostility and subsequent bitterness arising from the pro-/anti-treaty divide had not yet asserted itself. The voting papers had been segregated in the order of first preferences and placed in ballot boxes bearing the names of the candidates and the boxes were locked up in the counting hall. The exits and entrances were sealed and the doors were not opened again until the following morning.

When the count resumed, a Mr Bradley representing Labour was declared elected when his votes exceeded the quota. When the counting of the papers of Michael Collins – a pro-treaty Sinn Féin candidate, who had secured such a heavy poll that four ballot boxes had to be had to be utilised to contain the votes – the checkers found numerous invalid papers in the bundles. The count was stopped and Denis Barry as OC Republican Police, together with District Inspector Fitzgerald and Mr Jermyn, the Returning Officer, at once opened an investigation into the affair. The Republican Police had been on guard during the night and all the boxes were in the same condition as when they were placed in the hall the

Frongoch prisoners who later became TDs at the time of the Treaty and who voted for the Treaty and their constituencies (*Dáil Debates 1921*)

Michael Collins	Co. Armagh
Gearóid O'Sullivan	Co. Carlow and Co. Kilkenny
Paddy Brennan	Co. Clare
Seán Hales	Co. Cork (West, South, Mid)
Joe Sweeney	Co. Donegal
Pádraic Ó Máille	Co. Galway
Joe MacBride	Co. Mayo (North and West)
Michael Staines	Dublin North West
William Sears	South Mayo and South Roscommon
George Nicholls	Co. Galway
Séamus Dolan	Co. Leitrim and North Roscommon
Frank Bulfin	Co. Laoise and Co. Offaly
Pádraig Ó Caoimh	Co. Cork (West, South and Mid)
Dick Mulcahy	Dublin North West
Dan MacCarthy	Dublin South

Frank Drohan, Co. Waterford and Co. Tipperary East resigned rather than vote for the Treaty. He was mandated to vote for it by his Comhairle Ceanntair but as he was personally against the Treaty, he considered resignation the only honourable course.

Frongoch prisoners who later became TDs at the time of the Treaty and who voted against the Treaty and their constituencies:

Brian O'Higgins	Co. Clare
Joe O'Doherty	Co. Donegal
Seán O'Mahony	Co. Fermanagh
P. J. Cahill	Co. Kerry and Co. Limerick West
Tomás O'Donoghue	Co. Kerry and Co. Limerick West
Tom Derrig	Co. Mayo (North and West)
Dr. James Ryan	Co. Wexford
Domhnall Ó Buachalla	Co. Kildare and Co. Wicklow
Phil Shanahan	Dublin Central
Séamus Robinson	Co. Waterford and Co. Tipperary East
Séamus Fitzgerald	East Cork
Seán T. O'Kelly	Dublin Central
Charles Murphy	Dublin South
Dan Corkery	Co. Cork (West, South and Mind)
P. J. Moloney	Co. Tipperary (South, North and Mid)

previous night. Mr Jermyn felt that the whole election would be invalidated. A meeting with the election agents then agreed that Mr Jermyn would examine the alleged papers, 210 in total, and make a judgement on the validity of the votes. Denis put forward the theory that there had been no tampering but that some votes belonging to another candidate had accidentally been placed in Michael Collins' boxes. The situation was resolved and the final outcome resulted in the election of Collins with almost three quotas.

Between 28 and 30 June 1922 the Government forces carried out heavy artillery attacks on the Four Courts, leading to the start of a civil war, which lasted until 24 May 1923. The atrocities carried out by both sides during this period were to leave a lasting legacy of bitterness in Irish politics. The most shameful of these atrocities took place in Ballyseedy near Tralee, where nine Republican prisoners were tied to a landmine, which exploded, and the survivors were machine-gunned to death. The deaths of Michael Collins, Seán Hales, Rory O'Connor, Liam Mellows, Richard Barrett and Joe McKelvey and others robbed Ireland of many great men and women whom Ireland needed to establish the new independent state. The final overall casualty figures show the cost in lives of the Civil War:

800 Irish Government forces killed
3 Garda Síochána killed
2,000–3,000 (approximately) IRA killed
77 executed by Free State Government
12,000 taken prisoner

Civil War and Tragedy

Normal life in the country came to a virtual halt. All activity in the GAA stopped during the Civil War. A leading member of the West Clare Brigade of the IRA, who was also secretary of the Clare County Board of the GAA, was executed by Free State forces in January 1923. This murder split the GAA and for almost two years Clare had a pro-treaty and an anti-treaty County Committee. However, in County Kerry, a match was organised to assist in the selection of the county football team. John Joe Sheehy, a Republican, and Con Brosnan, an army captain in the pro-treaty forces, came together to organise a team. The team selected competed in the All-Ireland football final in 1924.

Following the Free State capture and control of Cork in May 1922, there was a mass withdrawal of active Republicans from the city. As a result Denis Barry was transferred to Wexford in August 1922 and was appointed to the divisional staff of the 3rd Eastern Brigade. He was arrested on 6 October 1922 in Courtown Harbour, County Wexford, by Free State soldiers in a general round-up of Republican Volunteers. He was sent to Newbridge Jail and thence to Newbridge Internment Camp, without charge or being brought to trial.

The internees were held in Kilmainham, Mountjoy, Dundalk, Tralee, Newbridge and Tintown 2 and 3. Denis Barry was first detained in L Block in Newbridge. These were old army huts without beds or heating and the long, cold winter led to inhumane conditions for the internees who had not been charged or convicted of any crime.

In the following letter to his sister Nora on 20 January 1923, Denis asks her to pay for any further expenses on his behalf until his return to Cork.

The Unknown Commandant

1014 Denis Barry
L Block Newbridge Camp
Newbridge
Co Kildare

My dear Nora

Just a line to say I'm alright and trust you are all likewise. I received your parcel quite safely some time ago also cash which you forwarded to me. If it is convenient for you during the week will you forward me £3 and be sure and keep a note of those monies as I will pay all back when I return to Cork. Also any other expenses you go to on my behalf for the time I am forced to be here.

I am so far alright in the way of clothing as I have all my own and those I needed I ordered from Mrs Collins, Douglas Street and got delivery of, I will settle this account myself on my return. This person sends me several parcels on her own, and now and again if you are in the city, would you, from me, leave her some butter, eggs as she has been awfully kind to me, as the Desmonds and if I should say all the old friends who have been good to us for the last 6 years are still kind to me. We certainly will have to thank a number of persons on our return for their kindness to us. I am very glad you got the frame safely as per letter just to hand. I was sorry the cardboard was not strong enough, but it does not matter in a sense as I have others made now, also some other items. I was really delighted to get your letter and to know ye are all so well, you can assure him I have just formed about the same opinion of the people as he has.

All the boys from Cork are here now, in fact any person who did any work for the Country for the past 7 years are as yet together here so I am wondering who is in Cork.

I expect ye will be very busy now for this spring, though in a way ye can hardly have any time to go on tilling as of old when matters are so upset, but we will trust in God and perhaps the ending will be as sudden as the beginning. Remember me at Douglas, Cork, Miss Lavallion, Miss Desmond, Hennessey,

> With sincerest wishes to ye all
> Your fond brother
> Denis

It should be noted that Denis quoted his number in the camp as 1014 whereas military archives informed the author his number was 10234. However, on further investigation it transpired that this number refers to another Volunteer named Barry who was released on 6 June 1923. This raises the suspicion that the official military records are open to question and shows how cautious researchers into the period have to be.

The death of General Liam Lynch from a fatal bullet wound inflicted by his old comrades, now members of the Free State forces, on the morning of 10 April 1923 as he retreated with members of his army staff to avoid an encirclement movement to capture him in the Knockmealdown Mountains, heralded the end of the tragic Civil War that had divided the nation. Lynch was Chief of Staff of Republican forces in a war he had done all in his power to prevent. As in the War of Independence, Lynch, a man with a good military brain, was a pragmatist who, where success was attainable, was prepared to fight on, while others of his comrades had felt that continuing the conflict was hopeless. There were growing differences among the Army Council during the past few months which caused Lynch serious problems. From an account by John J. Hassett we learn that one of his captors thought he was de Valera. He asked Lynch who he was and Lynch answered 'you did not get Dev, its Liam Lynch. Get me a priest and a doctor – I am dying. Bury me next to Mick Fitzgerald.'

Denis' next letter home from K Block in Newbridge was written to his brother Batt on 18 September 1923. This letter shows that some registered post to him did not arrive and he asks Batt to investigate this. He also asks for clothing and boots to be purchased and sent to him.

1014 Denis Barry
K Block Newbridge Camp
Newbridge
Co Kildare
18/9/23

Dear Batt,

I am sure you must be surprised at my long silence but circumstances over which at present I have no control accounts for same. So I am sure you will understand all without going into detail and at a further date I will explain. I received the letter, but the parcels I have not received since July 10th, will you put in a claim for same as if parcels are accepted by the post office, registered, they are fully responsible. See to same at once as it's a perfect scandal that such parcels have not been returned to ye or delivered to me. I trust ye are all quite well at home, Douglas and Cork.

I expected the weekly would be sent on from Cork as usual but I did not receive a paper since about July 7th, might you inquire if any papers were forwarded since then. I might tell you that I got a number of papers delivered to me about July 7th including the weekly carried for April 18th posted from Cork on 19/4/23. Now I will ask you to send me a good pair of boots. Size 84 bals (not derbys) medium weight, box calf leathers also a pair of Phillips Light weight rubber sole heels have the best quality and I will pay for them when I get out. I am very badly off at the present as my boots are gone. If the Central Boot Store is open, see the manager, Mr. Brown and he will likewise do for me. Those are about the two best houses. I will also need a breeches knickers but I am trying to get it from Dublin, as I want to get a good one, and the best houses in Cork being closed I could not get a decent one and there is no use buying rubbish. I suppose the harvest is all gone, as the weather is miserable, it will be hard to meet matters like this in the country, as what with bad harvest, bad prices it will not pay for the labour, but he who sends one year bad, sends another year good, so we have only to hope on. I hope Maggie is quite strong again. I understand she must be very worried over things. Be sure you register the parcel coming in and write me all news. Send a short note now and again as I am always anxious to know how matters are going on. Say hallo for me to friends in the country.

> Your fond brother
> Denis

Fasting or hunger strike as a means of asserting one's rights when faced with no other means of obtaining redress is something which has been embedded in Irish culture from the nineteenth century. This tradition reasserted itself in the struggle for independence in the twentieth century. The following instances are recorded:

1913: James Connolly went on hunger strike after attending a public demonstration in support of labour strikes. He was released after one week.

1917: Thomas Ashe, the President of the IRB was arrested following a speech he gave at an anti-conscription meeting. While serving a two-year sentence in Mountjoy Jail he joined a hunger strike which looked for the right of free association. Five days into the hunger strike, Ashe died as a result of being force-fed. Four days later the remaining prisoners succeeded in gaining the right to be treated as prisoners of war.

1920: The British withdrew political status and a hunger strike began in Mountjoy Jail in April. On 11

Civil War and Tragedy

August, in Cork Jail, sixty IRA members, most of whom were held without charge or trial, commenced a hunger strike seeking the reinstatement of political status. The authorities hardened their attitude and opted to risk the deaths of the prisoners rather than make concessions.

In the weeks that followed the British released or transferred many of the sixty until only eleven remained in jail. One of these remaining was Terence MacSwiney.

1923: In early October a hunger strike which had started in Mountjoy Jail, owing to a combination of jail conditions and a demand for political status, spread among prisoners in other jails and internment camps. Denis Barry was one of those.

Denis joined the hunger strike in Newbridge on 17 October 1923. Some verses from a poem by Pearse, 'Fornocht Do Chonac Thú', are appropriate to his decision:

Do thugas mo chúl	*I turned my back*
Ar an Aisling do chumas	*On the dream I had shaped*
'S ar an ród so romham	*And to this road before me*
M'aghaidh do thugas	*My face I turned*
Do thugas mo gnúis	*I set my face*
Ar an ród so romham	*To the road here before me*
Ar an ngníomh do-chím	*To the work that I see*
'S ar an mbás do-gheobhad	*To the death I shall get*

The Unknown Commandant

As the hunger strike progressed many prisoners gave up and there were newspaper reports that the strike had collapsed. Government propaganda served to bolster this view and Máire MacSwiney wrote a very poignant letter addressing the prisoners, which must have given some comfort to those who had given up and encouragement to those who persisted. (The letter is reproduced in Appendix 6.)

On 6 November 1923 Denis wrote what was to be his final letter to his brother Batt. Above all else, this letter shows his courage, his love of God, his country and his family, and his devotion to the cause that he and all his friends and comrades both in Sinn Féin and Cumann na mBan were fighting for:

My dear Batt

Your most welcome letter reached me last evening and no words I can assure you could be expressed in writing as to the consolation it gave me.

I hope there is nobody worrying over-much, as for the present, thank God, I am as strong as can be expected, not having eaten for 21 days, but otherwise can sit up in bed, and can get out while it is being dressed. The general state of my health, now at any rate, is really very good. I need nothing for the moment as friends I have by the hundred who attend me so my advice to ye is to do everything with a light heart, trust in God for His hand is greater than those who hold me here.

I got the parcel sent by Walter and Maggie which I am very thankful for. I know she must be worrying now, but try and impress on her not to do so. Remember me to the kiddies, Walter, Joe and Maureen. Tell Joe I'll give him a big surprise when I reach Cork, as please God I hope to some day. I wish also to remember all my friends, especially Miss Lavallion, Miss Desmond, Miss Wallace, Miss O'Brien, Mrs Collins, Miss Hennessey, and last but not least, Seán O'Hegarty who did a true friend's part during my stay here. I only wish I could thank them personally. If you can through him convey my dearest wish to the others of the old crowd, as one day the fulfilment of our desire will be achieved by other hands if not through ours, as only in that desire can you have Irish peace, prosperity, good fellowship and all that true patriots have given their lives for Erin.

Again wishing fond remembrance to all at home, especially my mother.

Ever your loving brother,
Denis

We can see from what was his last letter that both his will and determination were strong. He was still influenced by Terence MacSwiney's words on suffering and enduring and could possibly be said to have adopted the Latin motto *Fortitudine Vincimus* (by endurance we conquer).

Denis hoped to return to Cork to be with his family. The 'Joe' mentioned in that letter was his nephew, Joe Dain, who at that time lived in Douglas. He remembered all his Cumann na mBan friends and paid a special tribute to Seán O'Hegarty who was OC Cork No. 1 Brigade after the death of MacSwiney and had taken no part in the Civil War but who had made great efforts to bring the two sides together to end the carnage. Many of Denis' fellow internees were concerned about his health in his last week. Todd Andrews, also an internee, approached the prison chaplain and pleaded with him to have Denis moved to hospital, but his pleadings were in vain. The Free State Government's attitude, led by Cosgrave and Mulcahy, was to 'let them all die'. Both these men who had been comrades of Denis and the other hunger strikers during the War of Independence could not be seen to show any compassion to those they now considered to be rebels. On the other hand, what the internees wanted was to be kept in proper conditions suitable for human beings and not to be treated and housed like animals.

Denis' health went into serious decline from 12 November 1923. Rev. Fr P. Doyle, chaplain of Newbridge Barracks, gave him the last rites of the Catholic Church on Wednesday 14 November. His family in Cullen were advised that his condition was critical. His brother Batt saw him on Monday 19 November and had discussions with Commandant Hayes, the Camp Governor. Batt asked that Denis be removed to hospital but Commandant Hayes' reply was that nothing could or would be done for Denis as long as he refused food. Batt then sent a telegram to the Minister for Defence, Richard Mulcahy, stating that Denis should be moved to a nursing home, as his case was hopeless. The reply from Mulcahy was that 'no internee can force his release by a hunger strike'. Batt realised that Denis was not capable of taking food, so he signed a document stating that Denis should receive suitable treatment, including nutrition.

Denis was removed to the Curragh Hospital between 3 p.m. and 4 p.m. on Monday 19 November 1923. Batt called to the Newbridge Internment Barracks the following morning with his brother-in-law. He was informed that Denis had died at 2.45 a.m. that morning at the Curragh Military Hospital.

Officers of Cork Cumann na mBan. (Courtesy of Cork City Museum)

The Unknown Commandant

Denis' death was reported in the *Kilkenny People* on 24 November as follows:

Hunger-Striker's Death
Mr. Denny Barry, Well-known in Kilkenny, Dies After 34 days' fast

Denis Barry, Ballymartle, Co Cork, died in the Curragh Military Hospital at 2.45am, on Tuesday after 34 days' hunger strike.

He had been on hunger strike in Newbridge from October 19th, and on Monday afternoon was transferred to the Curragh Hospital, where he succumbed.

Mr. Barry was well known in Kilkenny. He was an assistant in the Monster House in 1916 and was actively connected with the Volunteer Movement. He was 'rounded up' and deported after the Rebellion. He was exceedingly popular in the City and his death is widely regretted, not alone by those with whom he was associated in recent political developments but by all to whom he was known, including those who are not in political agreement with his view.

No inquest to be held
Wednesday's Independent states – the body of Mr. Barry, who came from Cullen, Riverstick, Bally-martle still lies in the Curragh. The remains will not be handed over to the relatives. Intimation to that effect was made to a brother of the deceased by the military authorities at Portobello yesterday evening.

Civil War and Tragedy

When counsel for the next-of-kin visited Newbridge last evening he was informed by the Civic Guard that they had not been notified of his death. They then got into communication with the military authorities at the Curragh, and the latter informed them that the Provost Marshal had notified the Coroner, and that the latter did not consider an inquest necessary.

Mr. Barry's brother journeyed to Dublin last night, and it is possible that the relatives will institute legal proceedings in the High Courts today with regard to the holding of an inquest.

Very little information in connection with the matter could be gleaned by a special representative of *The Irish Independent* who visited the Curragh Camp yesterday.

The late Mr. Barry was removed by ambulance from Newbridge Internment Camp to the Military Hospital at the Curragh between 3 and 4 o'clock on Monday evening.

On Saturday, Mr. Batt Barry, a brother of the deceased, received a telegram to the effect that his brother Denis was dangerously ill and with his brother-in-law, proceeded to Newbridge where he arrived early on Sunday morning. Later in the day he saw the deceased, who was in hospital, four other hunger-strikers, including the Mayor of Sligo, being in the same ward.

'Denny was then speechless' said Mr. Barry, in an interview with our representative last evening, 'he looked up at me, and I think he recognised me. He tried to speak, but the effort was so much that he got into convulsions and became delirious.'

In the course of further conversation, Mr. Barry said the hospital where his brother was in Newbridge struck him as being altogether unsuitable. The floor was dirty and did not seem to have been washed. He drew the Deputy-Governor's attention to this matter, and said there would be little chance of his brother getting on in that place.

'The first intimation we had', Mr. Barry said, 'was this morning, when my brother-in-law called at the camp in Newbridge to ask how he was, and one of the soldiers then informed [him] that he had died that morning. He was also told to call back at 2.30 pm when full particulars would be given. We called back at around 3 o'clock and the Deputy Governor then told us he had nothing to do or say with the matter.

'I then telephoned the Curragh and I was referred to the Military Hospital. When I got to the Military Hospital they referred me to headquarters. At headquarters they told me telephone to General Headquarters in Dublin, and as I was speaking to them they referred me to Portobello.

'They told me in Portobello that the body will not be handed over to me.'

The late Mr. Barry was 40 years of age; he began his business career as a draper's assistant in Cork and was for a long period a charge hand in the Monster House Kilkenny.

A well known athlete, he was a member of the famous Blackrock hurling team which won the coveted All-Ireland Trophy. He was identified with the Volunteers since the early days and in 1916 was arrested in Kilkenny. Released after close on twelve months detention he returned to Kilkenny, and in the bye-election was a prominent supporter of President Cosgrave when the latter was returned in 1917. During the Black and Tan regime he was O.C. Police, 1st Southern Division, which post he also held during the irregular occupation of Cork.

The following chronology details the way Denis Barry was treated by the Free State authorities in those fateful November days in 1923 prior to and after his death.

Saturday 17   Denis' family in Cullen were advised by telegram that his health was critical.

Sunday 18   His brother Batt travelled to Newbridge.

Monday 19   Batt visited Denis in the internment camp. He saw his brother, who was lying on the floor, dying, and hardly recognised him. Batt then met with the Camp Governor, Commandant Hayes, and requested that Denis be moved to hospital. The Governor responded that nothing would be done for him as long as he refused food. Batt then sent a telegram to the Minister for Defence, Richard Mulcahy, stating that his brother should be removed to a nursing home as his case was hopeless. The Minister's response was 'no'. Batt, realising that Denis was incapable of taking food, signed a document for Governor Hayes authorising suitable treatment for Denis including food.

Denis was moved to the Curragh Hospital between 3 p.m. and 4 p.m.

Tuesday 20   Batt called to the Newbridge Camp with his brother-in-law on the morning of 20 November. He was informed that his brother Denis had died at 2.45 a.m. that morning at the Curragh Military Hospital.

Wednesday 21 Inquest by Coroner Dr. F. Kenna. (There had been some doubt as to whether there would be an inquest, but one was in fact held.) The Coroner requested that the body be handed over to relatives. After the Coroner's inquest Batt and his brother-in-law, Walter Dain, arrived at the Military Hospital with an undertaker, a decent death habit and coffin for Denis' body. There Batt was referred to Portobello Barracks who advised him that the body would not be handed over to the family despite the Coroner's order to release the body and they had to return to Naas and from there to Dublin.

Civil War and Tragedy

Thursday 22   The family instructed their legal team to act and Mr Patrick Lynch, KC, and Mr C. Maguire (instructed by Mr Ó hUaidaigh) attended at the private residence of the Master of the Rolls and made an application for the release of his body and for an order of *mandamus* to that effect. The Master gave leave to serve notice on the Free State Authorities to a hearing on Monday 26 November 1923. See below for a full press report of the hearing.

Mr C. Maguire BL was the legal professional whom Cathal Brugha had consulted about the formation of Republican Courts and the Republican Police.

Friday 23   Early on Friday morning the family contacted the Curragh to claim the body. They were informed that the Military were awaiting instructions. At approximately 3 p.m. that afternoon, they arrived at the Curragh and were informed that Denis Barry had already been buried by the Military at 1.30 p.m. at a site near 'the Glasshouse' even though a court hearing had been granted for 26 November by the Master of the Rolls. The family went to the grave and recited the Rosary and grieved for the death of Denis. Denis had been interned for fourteen months without trial or charge. In death he was now being kept from his family and comrades by a Free State authority, all of whom had soldiered with him for the attainment of Irish independence.

A full report on the inquest appeared in the *Irish Independent* on 23 November.

Prisoner's Death at Curragh
Inquest on D. Barry
A document signed by a brother

At the inquest on Denis Barry (38), who died in the Military Hospital, Curragh Camp, after 34 days hunger strike, the jury found death was due to heart failure due to inanition caused by his refusal to take food. 'In our opinion,' went on the verdict, 'deceased received proper attention from those in charge of his case'.

[*Author's note: Denis was actually forty years old when he died. The same error can be seen on the name plaque marking his grave in the Republican Plot at St Finbarr's Cemetery, Cork.*]

Bartholomew Barry, brother of the deceased, said he went to see his brother on the 19th and signed a document that the deceased should receive suitable treatment, including food. Dr. M. F. Kenna was the Coroner.

The Evidence

In his evidence Bartholomew Barry said the

deceased was a commercial traveller and lived in Cork. He was arrested at the end of September or October [1922]. On Saturday [19 November 1923] he was notified by telegram that deceased was dangerously ill, and every facility would be given to see him on personal application to the Governor. Witness could not say whether deceased was conscious when he saw him. He could not speak. He made an effort but got into convulsions. The doctor was sent for and witness left.

He again saw deceased on Sunday, and the doctor said he had given an injection. He told the doctor that, in order to sustain life, it was his wish the deceased should be given food. The next day he went again and signed the document (produced).

The Document

'It was a difficult position for me', said witness 'and there was a great responsibility placed on me. The man was incapable, and the surroundings were such that he hadn't a fair chance. I could not have his death on my conscience'.

Mr. J. Byrne (instructed by Mr. M. A. Corrigan, Chief State Solicitor) who appeared for the State, then read the document witness had signed in the presence of Seán Hayes, Military Governor on 19th Nov. 1923. It was to the effect that he was not in a state to accept or refuse nourishment and that it was his (Mr. Barry's) wish and he requested that his brother should receive suitable treatment, including food.

The Unknown Commandant

He wired the Minister for Defence [Richard Mulcahy] stating the deceased should be removed immediately to a nursing home, as his case was hopeless. He received the reply – 'No internee can force release by hunger strike.' He received the wire before he signed the other form. He did not discuss with the Medical Officer the advisability of having the deceased removed to a proper hospital.

In reply to Mr. C. Maguire (instructed by Messrs. Little and Ó hUadaigh solrs.) for the next-of-kin, witness said the doctor said, if given liberty to feed deceased by signing the form, he would feed him with suitable food. The doctor did not seem to like the idea when witness said deceased might run the risk of choking.

The conditions of the hospital, said witness, were not suitable for a man in such a condition. It was awfully stuffy, and the floor was very dirty and in such a way witness would not like to see anyone lying where deceased was. The place was dirty, the air was foul smelling and the clothing coarse and not fresh.

When the doctor asked him to sign the form, he told him that previous to that he had been giving the deceased stimulants. The deceased was a very strong athletic man, was a good hurler and walker and engaged in all classes of sport.

Governor's Evidence

Comdt. S. Hayes, Military Governor of Newbridge Internment Camp, stated deceased went on hunger strike on the 19th October. He had known deceased for several years. He did not appear to be so strong in recent years. The witness received a telephone message from a friend of deceased in Dublin asking for his requirements, and witness gave a list over the telephone. He was not in a position to know whether the things on the list were sent.

On the 18th Nov. he received a wire from the deceased's brother asking his condition and he replied as follows on the same day: — 'Barry not taking food, consequently weaker. — Governor.'

As regarded the statement of the brother of deceased about taking him to another hospital, witness said nothing could be done for deceased when he would not take food. The brother expressed his anxiety that his brother should live, and he was satisfied that his brother was not in a state to take food or refuse, he consulted the medical officer, and asked him would he be prepared to do what he could to prolong his life and save it, and the doctor said 'Certainly' or words to that effect, and the doctor and himself agreed that something of this kind was necessary and he told that to Mr. Barry. He then expressed the wish that food should be given to his brother and signed without hesitation the document (produced).

The deceased, said witness, was removed to the Curragh Military Hospital between 3 and 4 p.m. on Monday evening and he died on Tuesday morning at about 2.45 a.m. He could not agree with the deceased's brother that the place was dirty or the air foul.

The Unknown Commandant

Cross-examined

Cross-examined by Mr. Maguire, he said in the remark he made he meant that nothing could be done to prolong a man's life until he received nourishment.

And you held this document over Mr. Barry's head and said: 'Sign this or nothing will be done?' – I asked him if he would sign it, and I told him he would have to take responsibility for having suitable nourishment given.'

Witness was satisfied that the prisoner was being suitably treated. They always gave the best hospital treatment at their disposal, and whatever a prisoner asked for in the way of medicine was always given.

In reply to the foreman of the jury, the witness said the deceased up to the time he went on hunger-strike was in ordinary good health. The rules of the camp were that no visits were allowed to prisoners except by special permit, to be had from the Adjutant General. The impression conveyed by Mr. Barry's brother was that he would like to have him removed somewhere, and what witness meant to convey to him was that they could not remove him without the authority of the Minister for Defence, because they were of the mind that removing him outside would be releasing him.

The Regulations

Comdt. E. J. Doyle, Medical Officer, Curragh, gave evidence as to regulations issued by the Director of Medical Services in connection with the hunger-strike. In addition, witness visited all the camps in the area and he was in Newbridge every second day. It was his duty to see that the regulations were complied with, and they were completely complied with in Newbridge. He visited the rooms in which the prisoners were on hunger-strike. The room where the deceased was, was a large one and there were four patients in it.

The air was all right except the smell one always got where there were hunger strikers.

About a week ago he saw the deceased who was then decidedly weak. He also requested the senior physician at the Curragh, Capt. Boland, to attend to Barry in consultation with the other medical officer. The regulations were carried out in Denis Barry's case.

Captain D.L. Kelly, Medical Officer in charge Newbridge Camp, said he saw the deceased from time to time with Lieut. Langan. The deceased was going around the compound until the 1st prox. On the 2nd or 3rd Nov. he saw the deceased sitting at the fire. He asked him if he were feeling all right, and he complained of a slight pain in his stomach. Some days after that he finally took to bed, and from that time he saw him frequently and saw that he got proper medical treatment.

On Monday last he saw the deceased's brother. The latter said he would like that his brother would be removed to another hospital. Witness distinctly remembered telling Mr. Barry's brother-in-law where the deceased would be removed to. The deceased was removed between 3 and 4 o'clock in a motor ambulance and witness accompanied him. Witness gave the deceased stimulants on the journey.

Counsel – you gave him some food before?

Witness – yes, but not by the mouth.

Witness said that the ward occupied by Barry and three others was large and clean, well ventilated and with good light. The floor was clean and there were always smells in a room where there are hunger strikers.

As a medical officer he did everything to prolong the man's life short of forcible feeding.

The Removal

Cross-examined by Mr. Maguire, witness said the reason for the removal of the deceased was because the brother asked. He informed Comdt. Doyle as to the man's condition and they decided on Monday to have him removed to the Curragh Hospital. Witness thought he was doing all he could for the deceased by removing him, and in his opinion it did the man no harm to remove him. He had given the deceased cardiac stimulants, and he also gave him some nutrient enemas.

Is not that what may be described as forcible feeding?– His brother had given me permission to give him those. I did not give him any food until the brother had given me permission, nor did anyone at any time before Sunday administer a nutrient enema.

I suggest to you that Dr. Langan, in presence of an orderly gave this man what I call forcible feeding before the brother came on the scene at all.—He didn't, as far as I know.

To the foreman—I considered it was in his best interest to remove him to the Curragh.

They were forbidden by the authorities to forcibly feed a hunger-striker.

A Daily Record

Lieut. Langan M. O. stated that he was in constant attendance on the deceased. From 6th November he kept a daily record of his condition. He talked to him frequently about taking food. He always refused and that continued down to Saturday when he became unconscious. The cause of death was heart failure due to inanition, in other words, starvation.

Stimulants for Heart

Cross examined by Mr. Maguire, the witness said he gave deceased stimulants for the heart on Saturday, and he gave him an injection on Sunday.

He positively denied that he gave any injection before deceased's brother arrived. Witness denied that what they had done could be described as forcible feeding.

The administering of the nourishment in the way it was done required two or three orderlies and the operation would take place every few hours. There was other accessory work also to be done.

Another officer giving evidence said he thought the medical officers did perfectly right to move the deceased.

This closed the evidence.

Mr. Maguire applied for an adjournment for the hospital orderly in whose presence he said an injection was given before the deceased's brother arrived.

Mr. O'Byrne said there was a soap and water injection given for the purpose of moving the bowels.

The application was not granted.

Messrs. Maguire and O'Byrne then briefly addressed the jury.

Chief Supt. J. Maher, Naas, represented the Civic Guard.

Coroner and the Body

At the conclusion of the inquest the Coroner gave the relatives an order for the burial of the body, but on getting into communication with the military authorities, a request for the body was refused.

The following report of the High Court action was published in *The Irish Times*, on Tuesday 27 November 1923.

The remains of Denis Barry who died during the hunger strike at the Curragh Camp have been handed over to his relatives. It lay in Newbridge Town Hall last night and the funeral will take place in Cork.

In the King's Bench Division yesterday before Mr. Justice Pim in the case of the King (at the prosecution of Bartholomew Barry), vs General Richard Mulcahy, Minister for Defence, and Commandant Maguire, General Military Hospital,

Civil War and Tragedy

Curragh Camp, Mr. Lynch KC with whom was Mr. Conor Maguire (instructed by Mr. O'hUadhaigh) said that this was an application for an order of *mandamus* to issue, directed to General Mulcahy and Commandant Maguire, for the delivery of the body of Denis Barry, deceased, lately interred at the Curragh camp. In view of the events that had happened since his lordship granted leave to issue this notice of motion he apprehended that practically the only issue to be decided was the question of costs, and with a view to having his lordship's determination on the matter, he (counsel) was proceeding with the motion.

Mr. T. O'Sullivan KC and Mr. J. O'Byrne (instructed by the Chief State Solicitor) appeared for the respondents after hearing the affidavits and arguments in the case. Mr. Justice Pim said that it was not necessary now to decide the question of handing over the body. If he gave costs it would be a decision that the claim was a correct one. The order would be 'no rule and no costs'.

Later that day, 26 November 1923, the authorities relented and the mortal remains of Denis Barry were exhumed from the site near 'the Glasshouse' in the Curragh Camp where he had been buried and were handed over to his family. They were removed to a mortuary in Naas, from where his body would be brought back to his native city.

The funeral arrangements were to be as follows: Denis' body was to be taken to his Parish church, St

The Unknown Commandant

Finbarr's South in Dunbar Street, Cork. After reception prayers and overnight in the mortuary, solemn requiem Mass would be said and his funeral would take place to the Republican Plot in St Finbarr's Cemetery where he would be buried next to his fellow brigade Officers, Tomás MacCurtain, murdered Lord Mayor of Cork, and his successor in that office, Terence MacSwiney, who had died in Brixton Prison in 1920 after a prolonged hunger strike.

The remains of Denis Barry arrived in Cork on Tuesday afternoon, 27 November. However, the then Bishop Daniel Cohalan would not under any circumstances permit Denis' remains to be brought into any church in his diocese nor allow any of his priests to officiate at any religious ceremonies normally held when someone dies. He had publicly decreed this in a letter published in the *Cork Examiner* that morning:

> Dear Sir – I am not allowing the religious exercises, which constitute Christian Burial, to take place at the burial of Denis Barry. I regret very much to feel obliged to adopt this course. I knew the deceased; I knew him to be very interested in and to have a great knowledge of the social and moral question of the dangers that beset girls in Cork and all through Munster. I knew him to be a very good man. But if it were my brother that had taken the course that Denis Barry chose to take, I would treat his burial in the same way.

Dr Cohalan seemed to be much less assured of the moral

rectitude of his treatment of Denis Barry than his stern public utterance suggested. He wrote to the Bishop of Kildare and Leighlin, Dr Patrick Foley, in whose diocese Denis had died. He wanted to know whether Denis had received the last sacraments, as he felt he was unable to trust a Republican statement that he had. Fr Doyle, who was prison chaplain for Newbridge Barracks confirmed in writing on 27 November that he had administered the last rites of the Church to Denis prior to his death. For that reason alone it is difficult to understand the Bishop's decision.

We can also contrast the Bishop's attitude to the one he had adopted on the occasion of the death of Terence MacSwiney when he wrote to the *Cork Examiner* as follows:

> Dear Sir. – I ask the favour of a little space to welcome home to the city he laboured for so zealously the hallowed remains of Lord Mayor Terence MacSwiney.
>
> For the moment it might appear that he has died *in deficit*. This might be conceded if there were questions merely of the individual, but it is not true when the issue of the Nation is considered.
>
> Was Lord Edward Fitzgerald's death in vain? Was Robert Emmet's death in vain? Did Pearse and the other martyrs in the case of Irish Freedom die in vain?
>
> We are the weaker Nation in the combat. Sometimes we tire of the conflict. Anyhow, special questions such as the question of the land, of local government, of housing, of education, for a time engage our whole attention. But periodically the

memory of the martyr's death will remind a young generation of the fundamental question of the Freedom of Ireland.

Terence MacSwiney takes his place among the martyrs in the sacred cause of the Freedom of Ireland. We bow in respect before his heroic sacrifice. We pray that God may have mercy on this soul — yours faithfully.

✝ Daniel Cohalan Bishop of Cork

The bishop had also accepted that MacSwiney had received the last rites of the Church without confirming this with the Bishop of Southwark.

Seán O'Hegarty wrote to the *Cork Examiner* on 28 November 1923 in response to a letter from the Bishop of Cork regarding the receiving of sacraments by the internees, and concluded his letter as follows:

Finally there is Denis Barry over whose body these unseemly controversies were launched. He was my friend and I never hope to meet a man of more blameless life. But the only thing the Bishop of Cork has done is to place his name on that pinnacle where in our young days we found and honoured the name of Terence Bellew McManus whose body too was refused admission to the church at Queenstown from America.

There is also a strong suspicion that Bishop Cohalan had made his decision from the rather base motive that Denis had defied him in an incident following the burning of

Civil War and Tragedy

Cork a couple of years earlier. It will be recalled that Denis was instrumental in returning to Egans of Patrick Street valuable items of religious silverware consisting of chalices, monstrances and the like. When the Bishop heard about the theft and recovery of these items he insisted that they be returned to him for safekeeping since Egans' premises had been destroyed in the fire; but Denis returned them directly to the store management as soon as they had established temporary premises.

Terence MacSwiney has taken his place among the martyrs, Robert Emmet and Patrick Pearse, who gave their lives for the freedom of Ireland. Denis Barry also has a place in that exalted company despite the ban on his body being brought into Cohalan's churches.

Twelve months later the Bishop again showed his inconsistency by raising no objection to granting full access to funeral services to Volunteer William Healy.

Healy, who came from Donaghmore, Blarney, County Cork, had been executed in Cork Jail on 13 March 1923 for the unlawful possession of a revolver during an attack in Blarney Street. He was buried in the prison yard. Following many requests his body was finally handed over to his relatives on Tuesday 28 October 1924. His remains were first carried to Sinn Féin Headquarters at 56 Grand Parade in Cork city for the purposes of verification, as the authorities would not allow the coffin to be opened at the prison. The funeral procession, headed by the Volunteers Pipe Band, left the jail, followed by the chief mourners and a large detachment of Volunteers. The Lord Mayor of Cork, Seán French, and members of public bodies marched in the cortège. When the remains had been formally identified the cortège proceeded via South Main Street, Barrack Street and Lough Road to the Church of the Immaculate Conception for a short prayer service. The following day William Healy was buried after solemn requiem Mass. He had received a full Christian burial which had been denied to Denis Barry one year earlier. The Bishop seemed to have made the rules on these matters on a whim and not based on any Roman Catholic principles and it lead to complaints about him being made directly to the Pope.

A few years later, Fr Michael O'Flanagan a well-known priest with trenchant Republican views, speaking in Roscommon where he appeared with Éamon de Valera at an election rally, publicly denounced the official Church position on the Republican cause. He quoted Daniel O'Connell who had said: 'I take my religion from Rome but my politics from home'. Approving what Peter Golden had to say (*Oracles of God, the Roman Catholic Church and Irish Politics 1922–1937*, UCD Press, 2000) – 'that he would rather go to Hell with Denis Barry than to Heaven with the people who refused him Christian burial' – Flanagan wanted to go further, 'preferring to go to Heaven with Denis Barry, than to Hell at the head of a procession of high ecclesiastics'. The Peter Golden mentioned above was a cousin of Terence MacSwiney. He died in the USA and was buried in the Republican Plot in Cork on 19 March 1926.

Having been denied the benefit of a Christian burial, Denis' remains were taken by his comrades to the head-quarters of Sinn Féin at 56 Grand Parade which is

Civil War and Tragedy

adjacent to Cork City Library. The coffin was borne to the main meeting room on the first floor and placed on a table. The lid was opened and Denis' mother, aged eighty years, together with his brothers and sisters were allowed to grieve the death of their loved one who had died at the age of forty.

THE LATE COMDT DENIS BARRY

As a mark of respect to the memory of the late Comdt Denis Barry, all

Cinemas, Theatres, Dance Halls and places of amusement generally, are

expected to remain closed on Wednesday next, the date upon which the

funeral takes place.

TO THE EMPLOYERS OF CORK

Sinn Féin Executive

56 Grand Parade, Cork

During the period when Comdt Denny Barry occupied the position of Chief of Police in the City you made public your appreciation of his services in safeguarding property. Some of you wished to mark in a tangible manner the appreciation of the work he accomplished without fee.

On Wednesday Cork will mourn whilst his remains lie in the City. This Executive confidently ask you grant Comdt Barry's memory the last and only fitting tribute in your power – the closing of all business premises for the entire day.

AN RÚNAIDHE

Closure Notices. (Courtesy of Cork Examiner)

The Unknown Commandant

The rooms remained open all night and in orderly fashion, his comrades and his friends came to pay their respects. All night long prayers were said for the repose of his soul and for the grieving family. At 11.30 a.m. the following morning the rooms were closed to the public. His family and his closest comrades, including Seán O'Hegarty, David Kent TD, Máire and Áine MacSwiney, paid their last fond farewell to Denis.

The following report of the funeral was published in the *Cork Examiner* on 29 November 1923.

Late Mr. D Barry
Public Funeral in Cork
Impressive Cortege
The funeral of Mr. Denis Barry, who died as a result of hunger strike at Curragh Hospital, following his removal to that institution from Newbridge Camp, where he had been interned, took place in Cork yesterday afternoon, and was marked by scenes of a very imposing character. Well known through the south of Ireland in his business capacity as a commercial traveller, as a practical and ardent worker in the movement of the Gaelic Athletic Association, and as an active participant in the recent activation of the Irish Republican Organisation, the late Mr. Barry was held in the highest esteem and respect by a large number of acquaintances, and his demise under such particularly sad circumstances created general sorrow. Strict, though absolutely impartial, in the performances of his duties in each of the spheres

mentioned, the deceased possessed an attractive personality and a kindly disposition and enjoyed widespread esteem and respect. His remains reached the city on Tuesday evening and lay overnight at the headquarters in the Cork City Sinn Féin Executive at 56 Grand Parade. This unusual procedure in connection with an event of the kind was rendered necessary by the intimation of his Lordship, the Bishop of Cork that any of the city churches would not be available for the reception of the body.

For some hours prior to the funeral yesterday, large numbers visited the room where the remains lay and paid tributes of respect to the late Mr. Barry. The lid of the coffin was removed throughout each visit, which were continuous for a few hours and the queues that passed around the room, viewing the body as they did so, demonstrated the esteem and respect in which they held the deceased, as well as the sorrow that his untimely demise created. A public funeral was accorded to the deceased. The cortege assumed remarkably large dimensions, being fully representative of the business and political life of the city and county, as well as many parts of the country, as the funeral procession proceeded through the city it was generally recognised that it was one of the most imposing spectacles of its kind seen in Cork for some years. One of the outstanding features was the demonstration presented by managers of the Republican Organisation. That body of Volunteers as well as kindred units, especially Cumann na mBan, marched in full strength from the city and also the country districts, and its four deep solid ranks excited general interest.

The attendance of the general public and representative bodies was also remarkably large, and when it is stated that the cortege extended from the Grand Parade to Brian Boru Bridge, along the route followed its length and impressive character can be realised. The route followed was the Grand Parade, South Mall, Warren's Place, Brian Boru Bridge, MacCurtain Street, Bridge Street, Patrick Street, Washington Street, Victoria Cross, Dennehy's Cross, Wilton Road, and Lower Glasheen Road to St. Finbarr's Cemetery, and along each of these thoroughfares large numbers of people assembled to witness such an imposing funeral.

Excellent order was associated with the impressive proceedings, the public congregated along the route readily assenting to the wishes of the marshals of the cortege for a clear passage for the procession as the funeral proceeded along its sad journey. The public respectfully saluted the remains as they were borne on the shoulders of comrades of the deceased, relays being utilised in the observation, and at many points members of the Civic Guard and the National Army came to the salute as the coffin was borne along.

It was also noticed that in Washington Street members of the Civil Guard rendered valuable assistance to the marching marshals in keeping the spectators at such a distance from each side of the route as to secure a clear passage for the procession. Preceded by a number of volunteers, acting as marshals, the cortege was headed by the MacCurtain Pipers Band, which played appropriate music from the start to the finish of this sad journey. After that came members of Cumann na mBan carrying wreaths and the hearse, laden with beautiful floral tributes and on each side of which members of the Irish Republican Army acted as pallbearers.

This vehicle was followed by the coffin, borne on the shoulders of relays of the deceased's comrades along the different thoroughfares through which the procession passed. Prior to the transference of the remains from the Sinn Féin rooms to the funeral cortege the lid of the coffin was placed in position and closed by Alderman C. Coughlan and Miss Murphy, a member of the Executive of Cumann na mBan. Following the procession came the chief mourners and the representatives of the public bodies and general public, and afterwards bodies of Volunteers from all parts of the city and county, marching four deep, and large contingents of Cumann na mBan. The rear of the cortege was composed of carriages and motorcars, and all kinds of vehicles. The majority of the percussionists wore draped tricolour armlets. It was after six o'clock, darkness having set in, when the procession reached the Cemetery, and the final ceremonies promptly took place. By the aid of oil lamps supplied by Mr. Ed Donovan, the Superintendent of the Cemetery, who was almost indefatigable in his services in connection with the burial, the final scenes took place. A large gathering assembled around the

The Unknown Commandant

Republican Plot, in which the interment was carried out, while a massed assemblage congregated outside the main entrance to the Cemetery. Volunteers were on duty at many portions of the grounds as well as at its precincts and excellent order was everywhere manifested. The prayers at the graveside were recited by Mr. David Kent TD who, also prior to the burial, sprinkled the grave with holy water. Following the interment, during which many of the assemblage were visibly affected, the wreaths, numbering over ninety, were placed over the grave and after Miss Annie MacSwiney had recited the Rosary in Irish, Miss Máire MacSwiney TD delivered a brief oration. At the conclusion of these impressive ceremonies, some of the Volunteers sounded the Last Post and fired shots over the grave.

The chief mourners were: Mrs Barry (Mother), Mrs Dain, Mrs. O'Donoghue, Miss N Barry (sister), Jack, Batt, and Mick Barry (brothers); Walter Dain (brother in law); Joe and Walter Dain (nephews); Joe Mulcahy; Roger Ahern; Denis Conway; Jerh. O'Sullivan; Joe Walsh; Jeremiah Conway; Roger Conway, Mrs M O'Leary; Miss M. O'Leary; Mrs Sullivan; Miss Sullivan, Mrs D Conway; Miss M Conway, Miss M Walsh, Mrs J McAuliffe, Mrs J Conway (all cousins).

Three days after Denis Barry's death on 23 November 1923 Andrew O'Sullivan, an internee who had been held in Mountjoy Prison, died in St Brican's Hospital,

Civil War and Tragedy

Dublin. He had been on hunger strike for forty days. A native of Cavan, Andy was employed as a Department of Agriculture Inspector by the British Administration in Ireland and was based in Mallow. However, secretly, he was an IRA Officer and was a major source and conveyor of information for the IRA. His cover was blown when he was arrested with Seán Ó Túama who was on his way to America with important documents. Andy was taken to Mountjoy Jail where he joined the hunger strike.

Andrew's remains were brought from Dublin by train. He was buried after a requiem Mass on Tuesday 27 November 1923. The huge crowd present for the funeral was a fitting tribute to the great esteem and respect in which he was held. Volunteers were in attendance from the town and from all parts of north and northeast Cork.

The remains, enclosed in an oak coffin draped by the tricolour, were borne from the church to the hearse on the shoulders of eight comrades from the IRA, and were preceded by the officiating clergy and a large Cumann na mBan contingent, bearing floral tributes. He is buried in Mallow, which is in the diocese of Cloyne. Let it be noted that the religious service accorded in Andy O'Sullivan's case would not be allowed in the neighbouring Cork diocese.

A debate took place in the Dáil regarding the death of Denis Barry and the refusal of the Government to release his body. Among the speakers were Mr T. J. Murphy, a Labour Party TD from west Cork, and Thomas Johnson, the Labour Party leader from the Dublin County constituency. General Mulcahy was the Minister for Defence and a TD from Waterford.

The Unknown Commandant

Dáil Debate on the death of Denis Barry and the Government decision not to release his body.

Dáil Éireann – Volume 5 – 21 November 1923
Question on the Adjournment
Mr. T. J. Murphy *(Labour)*: I beg to give notice that I will raise, on the motion for the adjournment, the question of the refusal of the authorities to hand over his body to his relatives the body of Denis Barry, who died as a result of a hunger strike in Newbridge.

Dáil Éireann – Volume 5 – 21 November 1923
Question on Adjournment – Burial of Hunger Striker
Mr. T. J. Murphy: I gave notice that I would raise the question of the alleged refusal of the Government to hand over the body of the hunger striker who died yesterday morning to his relatives for burial. In any remarks I am going to make here I do not wish to aggravate the situation. I think that the decision of the Government, if the reports in the newspapers are true, is an extraordinary one, and I think it would be found that, so far as the opinion of the people is concerned, the decision is not a wise one. The decision arranging that this man's body should be retained by the prison authorities to be buried within the precincts of the prison amounts almost to this, that this man who has been an untried prisoner, and who has been in prison for twelve months, is to be treated as if he was an ordinary murderer. I do not think that that is wise, and I believe that every Deputy there and everybody in the country will agree

that the decision of the Government to permit the meetings of the Republican party to be held, to permit the Republican publications to appear, and not to interfere with the Republican propaganda, is a wise one. I believe if the Government are prepared to reconsider this question, and if we have a statement tonight to the effect that they are willing to hand over the remains, it will have a very reassuring effect throughout the country. I do not intend to elaborate this matter any further, but I think that we who have the reputation of being very generous to our dead and of giving them decent funerals will be establishing a bad precedent, if we deny our opponents the right to a Christian burial. In the county Cork the mother of the hunger striker is living. She is an old woman on the verge of the grave, and it would be very sad if this man's body were not allowed to go back to be buried amongst his own people.

Mr. Johnson: I would like to support the views expressed by Deputy Murphy. I think it is an unwise policy that, it is stated, has been decided upon. I hope it has not been decided upon by the Government. I think it would reflect badly upon their good-sense and general policy. On the lowest grounds, I think there would be very much more advantage taken to the detriment of the Government's good name by the refusal to let the body of an untried prisoner be taken home than demonstration, the fear of which is, presumably, the reason why the Government is said to have come to the decision not to allow the body of this prisoner to be sent home.

The Unknown Commandant

I think the case made by Deputy Murphy that he is an untried prisoner and that we have no right to consider him in the light of a criminal is sufficient to justify the demand that he makes that the body of his constituent should be returned to his home for burial. I do not think that there is any need for me to elaborate further. I simply add my earnest plea to his that the Government would reconsider the decision they have come to and hand over the body of Denis Barry to his relatives.

General Mulcahy: Much as the Government regret having to take such a decision as this, the fact is, that having all the circumstances in mind and having carefully considered the matter the Government have decided that in the case of any of the prisoners dying on hunger strike they will not hand over the body to his friends at this particular stage for burial. It is not a question of refusing a man Christian burial or burying him as an ordinary criminal. The remains will get proper and reverential burial but inside premises that are official premises. If later, when the circumstances are such that advantage cannot be taken of a funeral demonstration to prejudice the safety of the State or to jeopardise further the lives of men who are still hunger-striking in prison, the friends of Barry, or of any other person who may die in this wretched hunger-strike desire it, facilities will be granted to have the body of any such person transferred from the burial ground at present provided by the Government to any burial ground his friends or family may wish. The Government have to emphasise again the fact, that just now as at any other time, during the last twelve months or more when the safety of the State is prejudiced and endangered, it is their duty to safeguard the State. Every type of pressure that can be brought on men to throw their lives away in a useless protest, in a protest about nothing that can be achieved, is being brought to bear on men many of whom are generous men, generous as regards honour and general intentions but nevertheless a danger to the State, and the most unscrupulous pressure is being brought to them to sacrifice their lives in this particular way, and day by day, and week by week this, that, and the other inducement is held out by people outside who are unscrupulous in the matter, that if the men inside hold out another day or week, this, that, and the other thing will be achieved. The men inside were simply filled with dismay for having to adopt the situation that they had been forced into and they feel that instead of being ordered to continue the strike, the hunger-striker should be called off by those outside. Instead of that, this type of pressure is being brought to bear on them. In the circumstances the Government have decided not to put into the hands of those people who are working up this pressure the additional opportunities of funeral demonstrations that would have the result of sacrificing additional lives inside, and perhaps additional lives outside.

Richard Mulcahy was speaking with full parliamentary privilege and showed little or no sympathy on the death of a former comrade in arms.

The Unknown Commandant

During this sad affair the family were deeply aware of the hardship and disrespect shown to Denis' brothers Batt, Jack and Michael, and Walter Dain who was married to Denis' sister Margaret. Batt will always be remembered as a man of the highest integrity and for his resolve and determination to fight for the rights of his dead brother.

The hunger strike was over at this stage but the Minister for Defence Richard Mulcahy, despite his Dáil speech, still refused to hand over the remains. The Free State Government's former Volunteers in arms with Denis could not and would not be seen to have made a mistake.

In order to correct misstatements by members of the Free State Government appearing from day to day in the daily press, the following press statement setting out the facts and signed by M. Kilroy TD, Officer Commanding Mountjoy prisoners, was issued:

The Hunger Strike
13 October to 23 November

For over 12 months, in excess of 11,000 men and women have been held without trial or any hope of release.

1. The hunger-strike was started as a last resort against the inhuman conditions existing and was participated by free choice of each individual who went on it.
2. It was neither ordered nor recommended by the Republican Government of the GHQ IRA.
3. It has been carried on as it was started by the free will of each individual engaged therein.

The hunger strike spread to all locations where internees were held.

According to the *Irish Independent* of 27 November 1923 the sequence of events leading to the end of the hunger strike were as follows:

22 November 1923

Michael Mac Giollaruadh (Kilroy) [who] was OC of the prisoners in Kilmainham Jail wrote to the Military Governor requesting permission to send two delegates of the prisoners to all of the prisons and camps where there are hunger strikers, with a view to calling off the strike. For the full text of the letter see below.

23 November 1923

The requests were granted. Tom Derrig and DL Robinson who were interned in Kilmainham, visited the hunger strikers in Mountjoy, the Curragh, Newbridge and North Dublin Union. Mr. Hearty, an internee in Mountjoy, went to the men in Dundalk Prison. Resulting from these visits, all of the men on hunger strike decided to take food.

The following letter was received by the Military Governor of Kilmainham Prison:

Kilmainham, 22nd November 1923, the Military Governor, Kilmainham Prison.

Dear Sir, I shall be greatly obliged if you will

endeavour, without delay, to obtain permission from your authorities for me to send two delegates to those prisons and camps where there are hunger-strikers, with a view to calling off the strike.

In case this be granted I am desirous that the delegates should travel tonight and with the least possible delay, and that they be provided with a closed motorcar. I desire also that the interviews between my delegates and the prisoners' representatives should be private.

The delegates will give their word of honour not to attempt to escape if a guard not be placed with them inside the motor.

(Signed) Michael MacGiollaruadh OC Prisoners

The letter concluded with the note that the writer deputed Tom Derrig to call on the men in Mountjoy, the Curragh Camps and Newbridge.

The facilities desired by Mr. Kilroy were provided and during the night and this morning Messrs Tom Derrig and DL Robinson, who are at present interned in Kilmainham Jail, visited the men on hunger strike in Mountjoy Jail and the internment camps in the Curragh, Newbridge and North Dublin Union. Mr. Hearty who is interned in Mountjoy Jail, journeyed to see the men in Dundalk Prison. As a result of these visits all prisoners who were on hunger strike decided to take food.

In response to the appeal of his Eminence

Civil War and Tragedy

Cardinal Logue, reinforced by the later appeal of Professor O'Rahilly, I have decided to call off the hunger strike as from Friday 23rd November.

I ask that strikers in every camp and jail accept this decision and inform them that on learning that this has been done, the strike will be called off in this jail also. For the sake of Ireland and of the future, we must make this sacrifice as we consider that further deaths of Irishmen at the hands of brother Irishmen will only perpetuate unending bitterness in our loved country.

The following letter appeared in *The Irish Times* on the same day:

Sir – I would like, with your permission, to draw the attention of your readers in Dublin and throughout Ireland, and in other countries, to the fact that the number of prisoners at present being released is increasingly large, and the Released Prisoners Committee is greatly in need of clothes, underclothing, suits, and overcoats. A number of the released men were very delicate, even in a dangerous state of health and require warm clothing. We would greatly appreciate gifts to our canteen – tea, sugar, bread, butter, cooked or uncooked meats. Perhaps, friends who can appreciate what a good smoke is and what its absence means would send us a few cigarettes.

A little while and we shall see all our prisoners home. We want all the help we can get immediately. Subscriptions are really badly needed.

The Unknown Commandant

– Yours, etc,
Cáit Bhean Seán T. Ó Ceallaigh
Chairman of the Committee
Released Prisoners' Committee
6 Harcourt Street Dublin
November 26th, 1923.

This lady was the wife of Seán T. Ó Ceallaigh, later President of Ireland 1945–1959.

The family of Denis Barry received in excess of one hundred telegrams and letters from all over Ireland. Denis' mother, Nora, died in 1927, aged 84 years, with a proud but broken heart for her son who had given his life for his country.

The following article appeared in the *Kilkenny People* on Saturday 24 November 1923.

The Voice of the People
A Tragedy and an Error

The refusal of the government to hand over to his relatives for interment according to their wishes, the body of Mr. Denis Barry, who died on hunger-strike, has come as a shock to a large body of their supporters in the country. To show that they are a strong government, is, in present circumstances particularly a good thing; to show that they are a just Government is a better thing. To withhold from his relatives the body of one whom they loved appears to be alike an injustice to the living and the dead. The government had the right to hold his body when he was alive; they have no such right to hold it

Death certificate of Nora Barry, mother of Denis Barry, who died in 1927, aged eighty-four. (Barry family archive) when he is dead. It is impossible, when considering this question, to eliminate the fact that the late Mr. Barry was not convicted of any offence against the State; he was not even charged with any offence. The government in pursuance of the powers vested in them by the representatives of the people exercised the right to hold him without trial or charge, and we are not prepared to dispute their contention that in exercising that right they were acting in the best interests of the State. But we think it may very well be argued that with the death of the prisoner that right lapses. We are pretty confident the legislature, in authorising the government to arrest and imprison citizens without trial, never contemplated that their dominion would extend over their dead bodies.

One might be tempted writing in this connection to trot out the usual tag and to say that there is no country in the world where the dead are held in greater veneration than in Ireland. We refrain from doing that because we simply don't believe it. It is time to get rid of self-deception. A recent ghoulish affair in a mortuary chapel in Cork – an exceptional incident, no doubt – shows that a section of our people have less respect for the remains of the Christian dead than for the carcass of a mad dog and viewing the matter in another aspect; the condition of many of our graveyards is a scandal and a reproach that the responsible authorities show no disposition to end. Those whom we are concerned for in the case of the late Mr. Barry are his bereaved relatives who, apart from all political considerations, have a natural claim on the consideration and sympathy of decent-minded people. The fact that the funeral might be made the occasion of a political demonstration does not, in our judgement, offset the arguments that can rightly be advanced in favour of handing over the body. Are not these political demonstrations taking place daily in Dublin and frequently in every part of the country? The government rightly permit them to take place, and they do not seem to cut any ice.

Moreover, the government have won a signal victory in connection with the hunger strike. The hunger strike as a weapon against the government has been utterly smashed. The strike, in fact, has hopelessly collapsed and it is an outrage that the unfortunate fellows who are still carrying it on are not advised or ordered to give it up. With the exception of Austin Stack and one or two others, all the leaders have abandoned it. Mr. de Valera never entered on it. It is said that he acted on the 'advice' of his 'cabinet'! If the 'cabinet' were capable of advising him not to go on hunger strike, why should they not be capable of advising the less responsible men not to continue on hunger strike? General Mulcahy referred to the men who are continuing the strike as 'men generous in mind, in honour and intentions'. We endorse that statement although we believe they are being tragically misled. We think it was the present Governor-General who it was in his salad days – when asked to define 'nationality' said 'it was something that a man was prepared to die for'. Denis Barry had died for what he believed to be right, and we respect his motives although we cannot agree with them. He mostly believed he was fighting for a republic. He was not one of those who juggled with 'Document no. 2' – in which by the way, from first to last, the word 'republic' is never mentioned. He did not sign the Treaty (under duress), like Mr. Robert Barton; vote for the Treaty, as Mr. Barton did (was it, 'under duress'?) and then fight against it – also probably 'under duress'.

Denis Barry was only a man in the ranks. 'His not to reason why, his but to do and die'. He has died and we think that his relatives should not be denied the sacred right to paying proper respect to his memory, even if the occasion turned into a political demonstration. It is no consolation, but rather an added grief, to his people to be told that at some future time permission may be given to have the remains exhumed and re-interred according to their wishes. When the dead are at rest they should be allowed to rest. The future is with God – 'behind the dim unknown standeth God within the shadow'.

The Government have made a mistake and they should lose no time in remedying it.

A copy of the death certificate for Denis Barry issued after the inquest held on 21 November 1923. Note his age is shown as thirty-eight years, whereas Denis was born in 1883 and died in 1923, aged forty years. (Barry family archive)

6

In Memoriam

In the year 1920 there was, immediately inside the gates of St Finbarr's cemetery in Cork, a vacant plot of greensward in one corner of which stood a small but interesting memorial. Built in 1894 of stones taken from their ancient Abbey, it marked the place where the collected bones of the monks of Gillabbey had been re-interred.

On the day after the murder of Lord Mayor Tomás MacCurtain in March 1920, Fred Cronin, an intimate friend of Terence MacSwiney and a leading Cork undertaker, suggested to the Brigade officers that the Municipal authorities, who were owners of the cemetery, should be requested to make this plot available as a burial place for the dead patriot. The Corporation readily agreed, and with this first interment the Republican Plot came into existence.

In Memoriam

In the following years of conflict, the bodies of fifty-eight other soldiers of the Irish Republican Army were borne there on the shoulders of their comrades, to rest beside the remains of the first Brigade Commandant. Three who endured the pain of hunger strike to the death are buried there: Terence MacSwiney, Tomás MacCurtain and Denis Barry. Joseph Murphy, a volunteer who died in Cork Jail, is also there. 'To some who are buried there death came swiftly in the heat of battle, to others it came only as a release from torture or as the result of ill treatment while they were prisoners. Some too, although not buried there, faced the firing squads; others again were victims of midnight raids on their homes or fell to the pursuer's bullet on remote hillsides or quiet country roads.'

There is a 27-foot-high memorial, the work of Séamus Murphy RHA, made of limestone. The base, 12 feet by 8 feet, is a simple block with a carved recessed member having the following inscription cut on it:

Do Bhuanú Cuimhne na nÓglach
A bhain le Briogáid a hAon
D'Arm na Poblachta agus
Fianna Éireann a thug a nanam
Chun Poblacht Éireann a chur ar bun.

(Translation: A permanent memory of the volunteers who belonged to the First Brigade of the Republican Army and the Fianna Éireann who gave their lives for the people of Ireland.)

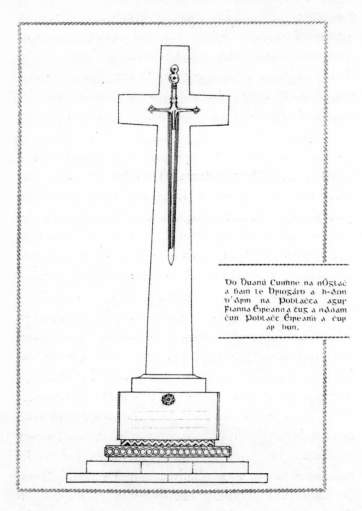

Do Ḃuanú Cuiṁne na nÓglaċ
a ḃain le Ḃriogáid a h-áon
d'árm na Poblaċta agur
Fianna Éireann a ṫug a nanam
ċun Poblaċt Éireann a ċur
ar bun.

Drawing of Republican Plot monument. (Courtesy of the Cork No. 1 Brigade)

In Memoriam

The cross is plain with well-proportioned tapering on front and sides. The arms also taper out, and the effect is graceful and dignified against the background. Carved in high relief on the cross is an enlarged replica of a famous sixteenth-century Irish sword which was found in the River Barrow, near Monasterevin, County Kildare, and is now in the National Museum. The design thus combines the sword as a symbol of valour and the cross as a symbol of sacrifice.

The memorial was erected by a committee representing all the battalions of Cork No. 1 Brigade. The committee was formed in December 1960, under the chairmanship of Seán O'Hegarty. The fund raised for the purpose had been contributed to mainly by surviving members of the Brigade, both in Ireland and abroad, with a notable and substantial contribution from those resident in the United States of America.

A number of memorials had already been erected in other places in the Brigade area such as that in what was formerly the yard of Cork jail, but is now part of the University College grounds, and where the bodies of men executed at Cork military barracks are buried. Some of the battalions have commemorated their own dead with memorials such as those at Midleton, Dripsey and Macroom. Sites of other engagements and deaths have been marked, as at Ballycannon, Dublin Hill, and elsewhere, but it had long been felt that the Republican Plot at St Finbarr's Cemetery, which contains the largest number of Brigade dead and which has such a prominent and public location, should be marked with a worthy memorial which would embrace all the 114 men whose names appear on the Brigade Roll of Honour.

There are sixty graves in the Plot, including three of the members of Fianna Éireann and three members of Cork No. 3 Brigade. Some graves are unmarked and on these the Memorial Committee hope to erect headstones.

The unveiling of the memorial by the then President of Ireland, Éamon de Valera, was arranged for St Patrick's Day 1963 at 3 p.m. Twelve hours earlier an attempt was made to blow up the memorial. The Republican movement denied having anything to do with the attempt but admitted that one member of their organisation was killed and another seriously injured in the incident. The unveiling went ahead despite the absence of committee chairman Seán O'Hegarty, due to illness.

In more recent times headstones for people not buried in the Republican Plot have been erected there. It is questionable as to who gave permission for this.

The unveiling of the memorial was reported in the *Cork Examiner* on Monday 28 March 1963, as follows:

President Unveils Memorial to Cork Patriots

Its damaged base so covered that the effects of the attempt made twelve hours earlier to wreck it with explosives could not be seen, the 1st Cork Brigade Memorial at the Republican Plot in St Finbarr's Cemetery was unveiled by President de Valera yesterday afternoon. About 6,000 people attended the impressive ceremony, defying the heavy rain which must have kept many more sympathisers away.

The decision to go ahead with the ceremony was

In Memoriam

taken after a mid-morning conference which considered amongst other factors the little damage to the memorial and the number of Brigade men coming long distances to attend.

The ceremony included the recital of a decade of the Rosary for the deceased members of the Brigade and when this had been said, Rev. Fr Eugene OFM Cap. who led the crowd in prayer, said: 'I ask you, in your charity, to join me in saying a decade of the Rosary for the young man who was killed in this morning's unfortunate explosion'. The men in the crowd bared their heads once more and prayed for the repose of the soul of the dead man.

There was a big turnout of the surviving members of the 1st Cork Brigade who paraded under Messrs Dan Healy and Con O'Connell and marched from Wilton Cross to the cemetery. A number of invited guests were seated around the plot in which Cork's two heroic Lord Mayors, Thomas MacCurtain and Terence MacSwiney, are among the fallen.

Before the ceremonies began, the Barrack Street Band played outside the cemetery. St Finbarr's Pipe Band led in the presidential party. The President inspected a guard of honour under Mr. Charles Brown on arrival at the entrance, and then accompanied by members of the organising committee, including Mr. Séamus Ó Muineacháin, MCC who presided (in the unavoidable absence of the committee chairman, Mr. Seán O'Hegarty) walked to the specially erected platform beside the new memorial.

The Unknown Commandant

Among those on the platform were Messrs Florence O'Donoghue, and George Buckley, Joint Honorary Secretaries; Joseph O'Connor and Dan Healy, joint honorary Treasurers; Tom Crofts; Michael Leahy, Tom Wallace, Mrs Máire MacSwiney Brugha (daughter of Terence MacSwiney), Mr. Rory Brugha and their two children and Col Brennan ADC to the President.

Blessing of Memorial

At the beginning of the ceremony the Tricolour beside the platform was flown at half-mast and the ceremony started with an oration from Mr. Ó Muineacháin. This was followed by the blessing of the memorial cross by Father Eugene and two decades of the Rosary.

The President formally unveiled the 27 foot high memorial cross by pulling away the covers over the inscription at the foot of the slender limestone structure and the Tricolour was then raised to its full height.

Brave Men of Cork

Speaking first in Irish and then in English, the President, who was greeted with applause, said: -
'Officers and men of the Cork No 1 Brigade and the people of Cork, I have come here representing the nation to assist in paying tribute to the brave men of Cork whose bodies rest there. May God grant eternal peace to their souls. Each one of them gave his young life and all its love and promise so that our nation might be free. And, it is only right that we, who are enjoying that freedom, should make sure

that the sacrifices of those who gained it for us should not be forgotten. The surviving members of the Cork No 1 Brigade have felt it a duty to see that this memorial which I have just unveiled, intended to signify sacrifice and valour, should be erected in the memory of their fallen comrades.

They and the people of Cork have reason to be proud of every name inscribed here. Two chief magistrates of their city, whose names are here, made the name of Cork City and Ireland and its struggle for freedom to be known and honoured in every land. The cruel murder of Lord Mayor MacCurtain, the first to be buried in this plot, and the long agony endured by Terence MacSwiney brought understanding of our cause and sympathy with it to every generous lover of freedom throughout the world.

The others who lie here and in many Republican graves in the country, they too, in their death and sacrifice, gave proof, as Terry MacSwiney did, that not all the armies of all the empires of earth could crush the spirit of one true man. Where the dead of Cork No. 1 Brigade may rest, the Memorial now erected in the Plot embraces them all. It is a tribute to their memory from surviving comrades and from the people in whose service they gave their lives.

Everyone who speaks in the presence of the noble dead as here must always find words inadequate. But it is perhaps right that I should point out to the young who are present here and have had no personal knowledge of the time, the prime circumstances in which these men offered their lives. Pearse and Clarke and Connolly and the other leaders of the Easter Week had in the name of the dead generations asserted, once more, our right to national freedom and sovereignty and proclaimed a republic. Later, on January 21st, 1918, the elected representatives of the people met in Dublin and gave formal democratic confirmation to this Republic. They set up Dáil Éireann to be its parliament and government.

The enemy then, in a campaign of 'frightfulness' set out to destroy the Republic and endeavoured by a regime of terror to turn away the people's allegiance to it. The Irish Volunteers who had now become the army of the Republic to protect our people's right to independence by the use of such weapons as they could secure. In the unequal fight, Britain with its empire then at the pinnacle of its power, success could only come through a firm determination on the part of our people to resist and not to yield.

Forever Remembered

It is for this determination that those we are honouring today will be forever remembered. We can best show our appreciation of what they have done by striving to raise for them a monument in the hearts of all citizens and by each of us playing his part so that freedom which they secured for us may be maintained, and our national individuality preserved. As we stand here by their graves should we not, indeed, in gratitude solemnly pledge ourselves, each one of us, never to weaken in our efforts to make our nation what they, with Pádraigh Pearse, would have it, "not free merely but Gaelic as well, not Gaelic merely but free as well". And so God grant that it may be.'

Go gcuidi Naomh Pádraigh agus naoimh uile na hÉireann leis sin a thabhairt chun criche.

Before his oration in Irish, Mr. Ó Muineacháin apologised for the unavoidable absence of the chairman, Mr. O'Hegarty.

Two-fold Purpose

After the blessing of the cross, Rev. Fr Eugene said that the gathering had a two-fold purpose. It was a public manifestation of the faith cherished since the days of St Patrick and it was an expression of the people's undying memory of their dead comrades and their unalterable devotion to their ideals. Unquestioningly the ideals of the fallen had been high and noble in which they worked, fought and died and they had been cast in a heroic mould.

Forty years after these men had fought and died for Ireland, the problems were different and more complex, but to-day no less than before Ireland needed men of high ideals and heroic stamp in private and public life.

A firing party under Mr. W Barry fired three volleys over the plot, and Mr. William Martin, of the Barrack Street Band sounded the Last Post and Reveille.

In addition to those already mentioned the organising committee included: Tom Crofts, Dan

List of Interments and Dates of Deaths

Cork No. 1 Brigade, Oglægh na hEireann

TOMAS MacCURTAIN	20th March, 1920
SEAMUS QUIRKE	10th September, 1920
P. J. McNESTRY	16th October, 1920
JOSEPH MURPHY	25th October, 1920
TERENCE MacSWINEY	25th October, 1920
CHRISTOPHER LUCEY	10th November, 1920
PATRICK O'DONOGHUE	23rd November, 1920
JAMES MEHIGAN	23rd November, 1920
PATRICK TRAHEY	23rd November, 1920
TIMOTHY CROWLEY	26th November, 1920
WILLIAM MULCAHY	26th November, 1920
DENIS C. MORRISSEY	26th November, 1920
JEREMIAH DELANEY	12th December, 1920
CORNELIUS DELANEY	18th December, 1920
EAMON TIERNEY	16th December, 1920
CHARLES J. DALY	1st March, 1921
WILLIAM DEASY	23rd March, 1921
DANIEL MURPHY	23rd March, 1921
DANIEL CROWLEY	23rd March, 1921
THOMAS DENNEHY	23rd March, 1921
MICHAEL O'SULLIVAN	23rd March, 1921
JEREMIAH MULLANE	23rd March, 1921
TADG O'SULLIVAN	19th April, 1921
STEPHEN DORMAN	23rd May, 1921
PATRICK BURNS	4th June, 1921
WALTER LEO MURPHY	27th June, 1921
CHARLES DALY	29th June, 1921
DENIS SPRIGGS	8th July, 1921
TADG BARRY	15th November, 1921
SEAN BULMAN	27th April, 1922
WILLIAM SPILLANE	30th June, 1922
WILLIAM O'SULLIVAN	18th July, 1922
JEREMIAH HOURIGAN	9th August, 1922
JAMES MOLONEY	9th August, 1922

List of interments and dates of deaths, Cork No. 1 Brigade, for the Republican Plot in St Finbarr's Cemetery, Cork. (Courtesy of the Cork No. 1 Brigade)

IAN McKENZIE KENNEDY	9th August, 1922
PATRICK BURNS	21st August, 1922
TIMOTHY KENEFICK	8th September, 1922
PATRICK MURPHY	12th September, 1922
JOHN P. O'BRIEN	14th September, 1922
JEREMIAH LONG	24th September, 1922
FRANCIS POWER	6th October, 1922
DENIS BARRY	20th November, 1923
GEORGE BOURKE	22nd December, 1923
JAMES HICKEY	6th April, 1924
WILLIAM MURPHY	4th May, 1924
DANIEL BARRY	10th May, 1924
LIAM CRONIN	27th May, 1924
LIAM HEALY	13th March, 1923
TIMOTHY HOBBS	18th November, 1924
CHARLES MURPHY	7th December, 1924
FRANK ELLARD	1st February, 1928
CONCUBHAIR O CROININ	17th October, 1930
SEAN J. KAVANAGH	3rd August, 1940

CORK NO. 3 BRIGADE, OGLAIGH NA hEIREANN

BARTHOLMEW FALVEY	15th February, 1921
SEAN PHELAN	15th February, 1921
PATRICK O'SULLIVAN	18th February, 1921

FIANNA EIREANN

PATRICK HANLEY	17th November, 1920
RICHARD NOONAN	11th October, 1922
JAMES PYNE	11th November, 1924

U.S.A.

| PETER GOLDEN | 19th March, 1926 |

Aꞃ Ueiꞃ Oé ꞁo ꞃɑıb ɑ n-ɑnɑmɑ !

The Unknown Commandant

Donovan, Seán Ó Luasa, 1st Battalion; Michael Murphy, Raymond Kennedy, Pat Collins, 2nd Battalion; James Ahern, Tim Herlihy, 3rd Battalion; Seán Kelleher, Jack O'Shea, 4th Battalion; John J Hegarty, 5th Battalion; Murt Cronin, Maurice Brew, 6th Battalion; Charles Brown, 7th Battalion; Patrick O'Sullivan, Séamus Ó Muineacháin, 8th Battalion; Henry O'Mahony, F Hourihane, 9th Battalion; William O'Connell, 10th Battalion.

Attended Mass

Earlier the President attended the 11am Mass at the Church of the Most Holy Trinity, Cork, yesterday. The Mass, which was celebrated by Rev Fr Celsius, OFM Cap., was offered for the repose of the souls of the deceased members of the Old IRA, Cumann na mBan, and the Fianna.

With the President were Major F O'Donoghue and Mr. Joe O'Connor.

Epilogue

This retelling of the life and death of Denis Barry was a very emotional time for the author and his closest family. Recollection of Denis' deeds and especially his final suffering followed by the refusal of the Minister of Defence, General Richard Mulcahy, to release his body remains a source of both pride and huge pain to his relatives. This final insult, following the death of a son and patriot, fostered more than a little bitterness and animosity in succeeding generations of the Barry family. As Deputy T. Murphy, Labour, remarked in Dáil Éireann in late November 1923, '. . . I think that we who have the reputation of being very generous to our dead and of giving them decent funerals will be establishing a bad precedent if we deny our opponents the right to a Christian burial. In the County Cork the mother of the hunger striker is living. She is an old woman on the verge of the grave.'

It seems bizarre that a hugely respected Corkman of his time could be largely forgotten. This omission may stem from a lack of archival material stored by the Department of Defence. The Department has no record of Denis Barry's Commandant position or his status among Cork Republicans at the time of his death. Allied to this, the lack of military recognition upon his death has ushered Denis into the pantheon of the Unknown. As stated in the foreword, it was a lack of public knowledge that led to this book. My sons have often reminded me of the derision they were subject to, when as youngsters they would tell their peers of their 'patriot grand-uncle'.

Within the city boundary there is no plaque or monument to Denis Barry and the many Corkmen who gave their lives for the freedom of their country. Where is the plaque that was on the Volunteers' Hall in Sheares Street? Future generations will not thank us for our failure to display and record the full story of the men, women and young boys and girls who together achieved in seven years what generations down through the centuries before did not, namely, Irish independence.

It is a poor reflection on Cork City Council that the Republican Plot in St Finbarr's Cemetery is not kept in better condition. Unauthorised headstones have been erected there in recent times for people who are not buried there and who had no hand, act or part in the War of Independence.

The legacy of the Unknown Commandant is one that needs to be remembered and commemorated. In a nation long since confused as to its identity, we need to revere the memorable and re-evaluate the terrible histories that are constantly being exposed. Ireland has a long history of insurrection and rebellion. The struggle for national

Epilogue

freedom over the centuries has led to the Republic we have today. Our native language and games are part of our identity as are our strongly held beliefs in free speech and the right for every nation to create its own destiny.

The Unknown Commandant is the story of the life of an Irish patriot, which seems overshadowed by the tales of more famous politicians and army personnel of the time. In saying that, it is a story that needs to be told because of the sacrifices made by hundreds of volunteers whose names were forgotten by the annals of time. Military records kept at the time have not helped preserve the memories of our fallen heroes. In Denis Barry's case, confusion surrounds arrests, charges and even prison numbers (see Appendix 9). According to the *Kilkenny People* of 24 November 1923, Denis Barry was referred to as being 'only a man in the ranks'. Upwards of 11,000 people had been held captive that year without trial or charge. Many of these people committed their lives to Ireland and its future without any recognition or plaudits.

The story is relevant to modern Ireland in the sense that some of the most important people in the history of the state have stayed largely in the background, much like Denis Barry, and left the limelight to the de Valeras and Cosgraves. Another parallel that could be drawn would be the sense of unity in Cork people upon the death of a respected and much revered Corkonian. In size and tone, the funeral cortège was similar to the occasions that previously marked the burials of Tomás MacCurtain and Terence MacSwiney and, in more peaceful times, those of Christy Ring and Jack Lynch. Denis Barry's death was at a time when Ireland was fraught with family feuds concerning the future of Ireland. His slow decline through hunger strike was exacerbated by the lack of decision-making that seemed to be going on around him and others. It seems that the death of MacSwiney a couple of years earlier struck more of a chord and precipitated more attempted action because it struck at the injustice of British rule. The British government did not hold the remains of MacSwiney for a number of days. Five years previously Denis had been the election agent for W. T. Cosgrave in Kilkenny and was a comrade in arms with those then in government. Despite this his death could not be honoured in a proper Christian way because of the cruelty of Bishop Daniel Cohalan and General Richard Mulcahy in particular.

Denis Barry gave his life for a free Ireland. He and thousands of internees, both men and women, who were inmates in the camps numbered doctors, TDs, Masters of Arts, legal personnel, and businessmen: people who believed that it was more honourable to be loyal to Ireland than to betray her.

Throughout his life Denis was a defender. In his sports career he was a defender of note both with his native Ballymartle and Blackrock hurling clubs. His Trade Union action shows that he was a defender of workers' rights and, even when he was self-employed, he continued his active participation in the Trade Union movement. In 1914 he joined the Volunteers to defend his country against the enemy. He was loyal to his leaders and, when he was assigned to Kilkenny to help and organise, he showed his dedication. His imprisonment in Kilkenny Jail and Richmond Barracks and subsequent

Epilogue

internment in Frongoch camp did not diminish his determination or his resolve.

Denis Barry served the citizens of Cork when, as OC Republican Police, he defended them from law-breakers who used the chaos of the times to take advantage of the lack of law and order. He returned stolen property to its rightful owners and ensured that people could walk the streets of the city in relative safety. He again showed his best qualities when, during his internment in Tintown, Newbridge, and after twelve months without charge or trial, he joined the hunger strike to demand and defend the right to be treated as a human being no different from those who detained him and who a few short years earlier had been his comrades in arms.

Batt Barry, brother of Commandant Denis Barry, unveiling a plaque in honour of his brother in 1966 in Riverstick, County Cork. (Courtesy of Cork Examiner)

The Unknown Commandant

Denis campaigned in Kilkenny for William Cosgrave in that man's successful attempt to be elected to the first Dáil Éireann. Cosgrave and his government cast him and thousands of his comrades into horse stables. He was left to die and his remains refused to his family. The Free State government did not want any show of public respect for his funeral in the same way that the British would not allow the remains of Terence MacSwiney pass through Dublin three years earlier.

Such is the man to whom this book is dedicated. History has ignored him. Most of the history books written about that time contain just a comment about the death of a hunger striker in the Curragh Camp. His remains are buried next to his fellow Commandants, Terence MacSwiney and Tomás MacCurtain, in St Finbarr's Cemetery, Cork, and no other monument or plaque in his honour exists in Cork city.

Terence MacSwiney and Tomás MacCurtain have been commemorated by street names and place names in Ireland and in countries far beyond these shores. Surely it must be right that we should remember our own Volunteers with other than what is written in song and remembered in folklore? With the centenary of the 1916 Rising fast approaching it would be fitting and appropriate that a memorial be erected in Cork city to remember both the fallen and the Volunteers who lived on to foster the future of a fledgling nation. I would like this memorial to show the various battalions that constituted the Cork No. 1 Brigade, Óglaigh na hÉireann, with the names of every Volunteer, Cumann na mBan and Fianna Éireann member inscribed. It would

Epilogue

be entirely appropriate if this memorial was erected outside the old Sinn Féin office on the Grand Parade.

I, Donnachadh de Barra, namesake and nephew of Denis Barry, am proud of him and his comrades who are now forgotten and hope that historians will grant him rightful place in Irish history and include him in the celebrations of the independence of our country for which he gave his life.

Ar dheis Dé go raibh a anam dílis.

Appendix 1

Roll of Honour of Cork No. 1 Brigade, Óglaigh na hÉireann and map of Cork No. 1 Brigade area

Roll of Honour

Cork No. 1 Brigade, Oglaigh na h-Eireann

BRIGADE STAFF

TOMAS MacCURTAIN	20th March, 1920
TERENCE MacSWINEY	25th October, 1920
DENIS BARRY	20th November, 1923

FIRST BATTALION

TADG BARRY	15th November, 1921
SEAN BULMAN	27th April, 1922
PATRICK BURNS	4th June, 1921
DANIEL CROWLEY	23rd March, 1921
TIMOTHY CROWLEY	26th November, 1920
LIAM CRONIN	27th May, 1924
WILLIAM DEASY	23rd March, 1921
THOMAS DENNEHY	23rd March, 1921
JEREMIAH DELANEY	12th December, 1920
CORNELIUS DELANEY	18th December, 1920
FRANK ELLARD	1st February, 1928
LIAM HEALY	13th March, 1923
JEREMIAH HOURIGAN	9th August, 1922
TIMOTHY KENEFICK	8th September, 1922
CHRISTOPHER LUCEY	10th November, 1920
JAMES MOLONEY	9th August, 1922
DENIS C. MORRISSEY	26th November, 1920
LIAM MULCAHY	26th November, 1920
JEREMIAH MULLANE	23rd March, 1921
DANIEL MURPHY	23rd March, 1921
WILLIAM MURPHY	18th December, 1918
PATRICK MURPHY	9th September, 1922
WILLIAM MURPHY	4th May, 1924
DANIEL McCARTHY	20th August, 1922
CONCUBHAIR O CROININ	17th October, 1930
JOHN O'BRIEN	31st July, 1920
SEAN O'DONOGHUE	28th September, 1922
CHRISTOPHER OLDEN	12th August, 1922
MICHAEL O'SULLIVAN	23rd March, 1921
WILLIAM O'SULLIVAN	18th July, 1922
MATTHEW RYAN	29th March, 1923
DENIS SPRIGGS	8th July, 1921
MICHAEL TOBIN	20th May, 1919

The Unknown Commandant

SECOND BATTALION

GEORGE BOURKE	22nd December, 1923
DANIEL BARRY	10th May, 1924
PATRICK BURNS	21st August, 1922
CHARLES J. DALY	29th June, 1921
CHARLES DALY	1st March, 1921
STEPHEN DORMAN	23rd May, 1921
TIMOTHY HOBBS	18th November, 1924
JEREMIAH LONG	24th September, 1922
P. J. McNESTRY	16th October, 1920
CHARLES MURPHY	7th December, 1924
JOSEPH MURPHY	25th October, 1920
JAMES MEHIGAN	23rd November, 1920
JOHN O'BRIEN	14th September, 1922
PATRICK O'DONOGHUE	23rd November, 1920
TADG O'SULLIVAN	19th April, 1921
SEAMUS QUIRKE	9th September, 1920
WILLIAM SPILLANE	30th June, 1922
EAMON TIERNEY	16th December, 1920
PATRICK TRAHEY	23rd November, 1920

THIRD BATTALION

JAMES FOLEY	1st April, 1921
WALTER LEO MURPHY	27th June, 1921
JEREMIAH O'HERLIHY	11th October, 1920

FOURTH AND TENTH BATTALIONS

JEREMIAH AHERN	20th February, 1921
LIAM AHERN	20th February, 1921
JAMES AHERN	20th February, 1921
JOHN AHER	16th June, 1920
WILLIAM BRANSFIELD	17th May, 1921
WILLIAM COX	25th October, 1922
SEAN DEASY	15th February, 1922
DONAL DENNEHY	20th February, 1921
MICHAEL DESMOND	20th February, 1921
DAVID DESMOND	20th February, 1921
MICHAEL FITZGERALD	25th January, 1923
MICHAEL JOSEPH GEELAN	10th October, 1921
JAMES GLAVIN	20th February, 1921
DANIEL HALLORAN	22nd October, 1922
MICHAEL HALLIHANE	20th February, 1921
WILLIAM HEFFERNAN	27th January, 1920
RICHARD HEGARTY	20th February, 1921
WILLIAM HOARE	8th April, 1921
DERMOT HURLEY	28th May, 1921

Appendix 1

JOHN JOSEPH JOYCE	20th February, 1921
MAURICE MOORE	28th February, 1921
JOSEPH MORRISSEY	20th February, 1921
PATRICK MORRISSEY	9th April, 1920
WILLIAM P. O'BRIEN	28th November, 1916
PATRICK O'REILLY	25th January, 1923
PATRICK O'SULLIVAN	28th February, 1921
JAMES MARY QUAIN	10th May, 1921
JOSEPH REID	29th September, 1918
DENIS RING	9th November, 1920
CHRISTOPHER O'SULLIVAN	20th February, 1921

FIFTH BATTALION

WILLIAM BUCKLEY	26th September, 1922

SIXTH BATTALION

JAMES BARRETT	22nd March, 1921
DENIS CREEDON	15th September, 1922
PETER O'CALLAGHAN	28th February, 1921
PATRICK O'MAHONY	28th February, 1921
FRANCIS POWER	28th February, 1921
JOHN LYONS	28th February, 1921
TIMOTHY McCARTHY	15th May, 1921
THOMAS O'BRIEN	28th February, 1921
DANIEL O'CALLAGHAN	6th October, 1922

SEVENTH BATTALION

DANIEL BUCKLEY	8th June, 1921
JAMES BUCKLEY	15th September, 1922
JEREMIAH CASEY	5th December, 1922
DENIS CREEDON	14th September, 1922
CORNELIUS FOLEY	6th March, 1921
MICHAEL GALVIN	27th August, 1920
WILLIAM HARRINGTON	27th July, 1922
TIMOTHY O'LEARY	4th November, 1922
PATRICK O'MAHONY	17th July, 1922

EIGHTH BATTALION

LIAM HEGARTY	5th September, 1920
IAN McKENZIE KENNEDY	9th August, 1922
JEREMIAH CASEY	2nd January, 1921

NINTH BATTALION

JAMES HICKEY	6th April, 1924
MICHAEL JOHN O'MAHONY	28th February, 1921

FIANNA EIREANN

PATRICK HANLEY	17th November, 1920
RICHARD NOONAN	11th October, 1922
JAMES PYNE	11th November, 1924.
SEAMUS COURTNEY	22nd July, 1918

The Unknown Commandant

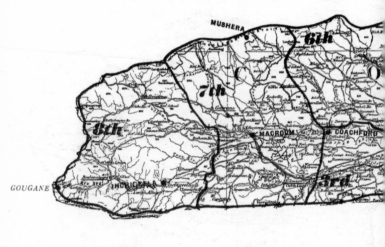

Map of Cork Brigade Area. (Courtesy of Cork No. 1 Brigade)

Appendix 1

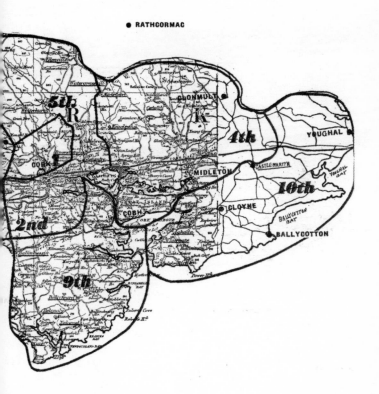

Appendix 2

Prison Memoirs from the *Kilkenny People*, **8 July 1916 (written by Mossie Higgins)**

Were you ever in gaol! If not you had better keep within the law. But you are not within the law now-a-days if you are sympathetically inclined towards the legal organisations known as the Irish Volunteers, the Gaelic Association or the Gaelic League. In fact, any Irishman, exercising the free will, reason and understanding that God endowed all mankind with, happening to be in Kilkenny on the 5th May last, was open to arrest. Such was the fact of some thirty law-abiding Kilkenny men the memorable 5th May last. The answer to the natural question, 'What is the charge?' (which is never denied the lowest criminal), was a presentation of fixed bayonets, a stern command 'About Turn'.

Once inside prison walls, all precautions were duly taken for our safety. A cell, 13.5 x 6.5 feet with little or

The Unknown Commandant

no ventilation was to be our temporary abode and an observance of rules, which were never forced on the lowest criminal, our lot. In this cell, one slept, ate food (not enough for a dog) and dwelt for 72 hours within the narrow confines of this abode and not allowed out to take even one mouthful of God's pure air, which the beasts of the field freely breathe. Nor was this all. Ordinary sanitary accommodation was time and again denied. These were the conditions under which we existed in Kilkenny Prison and the writer defies refutation. That the poor fellow o'er whose grave the grass now grows green, was hastened to his death by 24 hours of such treatment, there can be little or no doubt.

Appendix 3

List of Irish prisoners detained at Frongoch, Wales

T he following is a partial list of prisoners taken from the Prisoners' Camp Register maintained by the General Council. For example, some internees who were detained from late July onwards are not recorded (because they were released very soon afterwards). The handwriting in the Roll Book is occasionally poor which may account for some misspellings. However, it is a superior record to that listed in *The Irish Times'* *Handbook of the Rebellion*, where many pertinent details such as names, townlands and towns are misspelled and many names are repeated.

Note the names of Tomás MacCurtain, Terence MacSwiney and Denis Barry are included in this list.

County Antrim, All Belfast
Barnes, Jerry, 66 St James Park.
Bootle, Frank, Alexander Street West.

The Unknown Commandant

Burns, Peter, 7 Linden St.

Carolan, Mick, 80 Chief St.

Clear, Thomas J., 57 Agincourt Ave.

Connolly, Alex J., 2 Alamanda Tce.

Cotton, Alfie, 2 Rosemount Gardens.

Dempsey, Patrick, 40 Lorcan St, Broadway.

Dobbyn, Seamus, 21 Clonard Gardens.

Haskin, Robert c/o 56 Coolfin St, Donegal Rd

Heron, Sam, Doris St

Johnston, James, Sandown Rd, Knock.

Kelly, John, Irish Street.

McCullough, Denis, Grosvenor Rd.

McDowell, Charles, 19 Lorcan Street.

Nash, Pat, 52 Gibson St.

Neeson, Seán, 153 Falls Rd.

Osbourne, Harry, 69 Smithfield.

Shannon, Cathal, 27 Canning Street.

Smith, James, 3 Somerville Gardens.

Tierney, Edward, Falls Rd.

Wilson, Thomas, 248 Albert Bridge Rd.

County Armagh
Donnelly, Michael, Silverbridge.

County Carlow
O'Donoghue, W. P. Clonmore, Hacketstown.

County Cavan
Codwell, Pat, Carrackboy.

O'Reilly, Luke, Ballyjamesduff.

County Clare
Brennan, Michael, Meelick.

Brennan, Patrick, Meelick.

Appendix 3

Canny, Daniel, Tulla.
Dynan, Mick, O'Callaghan, Mills.
Healy, Denis, Bodyke.
Kelly, Timothy, Feakle.
Malone, J. Ard Feakle,
O'Connor, Patrick, Killaloe.
O'Donnell, Arthur, Tullycrine.
O'Halloran, C. Tulla.
O'Loughlin, Thomas, Ennistymon.

County Cork

Ahern, Con, Dunmanway.
Ahern, Maurice, Dungourney.
Barrett, Edward, Ballinadee.
Barrett, Edward, Kilbrittain.
Browne, Charles, Macroom.
Buckley, James, Millstreet.
Carmody, Patrick, Millstreet.
Casey, William, Mitchelstown.
Collins, John, Ballinadee
Corkery, Daniel, Macroom.
Cronin, John, Macroom.
Crowley, John, Glandore.
Crowley, Timothy, Glandore.
DeBarra, Tomas, Rathluirc.
Duggan, William, Dunmanway.
Foley, Joseph, Eyeries.
Griffin, Michael, Ballinadee.
Hales, John, Ballinadee.
Hales, Robert, Bandon.
Hales, William, Ballinadee.
Hannigan, James, Mitchelstown.
Harrington, Daniel, Macroom.

The Unknown Commandant

Healy, Matthew, Bandon.
Hegarty, Daniel, J., Mallow.
Hyde, Michael, Ballinhassig.
Hyde, Patrick, Ballinhassig.
Kinery, Martin, Fermoy.
Lorgan, John, Baltimore.
Lorgan, John, Baltimore.
Lynch, John, Macroom.
Lynch, Michael F., Ballyfeard.
Lynch, Tim, Ballyfeard.
Manning, Daniel, Kilbrittain.
Manning, Denis, Kilbrittain.
McCarthy, Daniel, Dunmanway
Murphy, John, Lissarda.
O'Connor, Patrick, Macroom.
O'Brien, John, Fermoy.
O'Callaghan, Con, Millstreet.
O'Connell, Christopher, Mallow.
O'Connor, Stephen, Macroom.
O'Dea, John, Rathluirc.
O'Donoghue, Con, Ballinadee.
O'Donoghue, Pat, Ballinadee.
Ó hEadamhain, Lorcan, Rathluric.
O'Hourihan, John, Skibbereen.
O'Leary, John, Ballinhassig.
O'Mahony, Con, Enniskeane.
O'Shea, Patrick, Fermoy.
O'Shea, Tadhg, Dunmanway.
O'Sullivan, M. Mitchlestown.
O'Sullivan, Patrick, Mitchlestown.
Quill, Michael, Macroom.
Reardon, Jehr, Millstreet.
Reardon, John, Ballywick.

Appendix 3

Reardon, Tim, Ballyboy.
Roche, Pat, Mitchlestown.
Spillane, John, Fermoy.
Sullivan, Con, Dunmanway.
Twomey, Jehr, Millstreet.

Cork City
Begley, Joseph, Castle Rd.
Collins, David, Bollards Lane.
De Courcey, Albert, 31 Geraldine Place.
Harris, Michael J., Tower St.
Hennessy, William, 34 Popes Quay.
MacCurtain, Thomas, Davis St.,
MacSwiney, Terence, 4 Grand View Tce.
McEnright, D. J., 4 Waterloo Tce.
Richardson, Joseph, Ashgrove, Togher.
Walsh, Tom, 13 Henry Street.

County Kildare
Harris, Thomas, Prosperous.
Maguire, Thomas, Maynooth.
O'Buachalla, Domhnall, Maynooth.
O'Reagain, Liam, Maynooth.
O'Ryan, Oliver, Maynooth.
Tyrrell, Tim, Maynooth.

County Kilkenny
Barry, Denis, Kilkenny City (native of Cork).
Denn, William, Talbots Inch.
Healy, Richard, J., Jenkinstown.
Lalor, James, Kilkenny City.
O'Shea, John, Knocktopher.
Treacy, Thomas, Kilkenny City.

The Unknown Commandant

County Laois
Fawley, John, Wolfhill.

County Leitrim
Daly, John, Manorhamilton.
Dolan, James, Manorhamilton.
Maguire, Bernard, Glenfarne.
McElgunn, Thomas, Manorhamilton.
O'Loughlin, Thomas, Manorhamilton.

County Limerick
Armstrong, James, Galbally.
Dore, Eamon T., Glin.
Gaffney, J., Kilmallock.
McInerney, Thomas, 10 Lock Quay. City.
McNamara, S., Loghill.
Nestor, Seán, 25 Edward St. City.
O'Briain, Liam P., Galbally.
O'Flanagan, Matt, Newcastle West.
Quigley, James, 3 Garryowen, Cottages, Limerick City.
Ruttle, Sam, Adare.

County Longford
Cahill Wilson, H. J., Longford Town.
Connaghton, Pat, Longford Town.
Curran, James, Newtownbarry.
Cusack, Paul Dawson, Granard.
Doyle, Patrick, Granard.
Farrell, James, Whitehall.
MacAmhalgaidh, S., Granard.
McGrath, Michael, Keenagh.

Appendix 3

County Louth

Atkinson, William, Dundalk.

Barrett, John, Dundalk.

Berrill, Patrick Joseph, Dundalk.

Burke, Thomas, Drogheda.

Clifford, Peter, Dundalk.

Donnelly, Patrick, Carlingford.

Farrelly, James, Ardee.

Ferguson, Michael, Carlingford

Hanlon, James, Carlingford.

Finnegan, Joseph, Drogheda.

Finnegan, John, Dundalk.

Hall, Samuel, Dundalk.

Halpin, Peter, Dundalk.

Hamill, Thomas, Dundalk.

Jennings, James, Dundalk.

Keenan, Michael J., Drogheda.

Mathews, Thomas, Ardee.

Appendix 4

Tribute to Denis Barry from *Eire Nua* – *The Irish Nation*, 1 December 1923

(Translated into English with the help of Criostóir de Baróid)

Bhí an píosa seo sa pháipéir *Éire Nua* – *The Irish Nation* ar an chéad lá de Mí na Nollag 1923.

Donnchadh de Barra

Ceann-oide Piléri na Poblochta i gCorcaigh a beadh an fear seo agus in a theannta sin cara cléibhe le Toirdealbhach mac Suibhne agus Tomás mac Curtain. D'oibrigh se le Toirdealbhach agus in a dhiadh sin do lean se ar a chuid saothar ar chuma fé ndear morán molata ó Cómhaltas Chorcaighe. Nuair do thainigh lucht an tSaorstáit go Corcaigh do thógadar furmhor na bhfear dar bhailigh sé le cherle agus gach a raibh déanta aige le h-aghaidh siochána na cathrach. Do bhí se fé mheas agus onóir ag gach aoinne go raibh ainthe acu air.

The Unknown Commandant

The above item written in Irish was published in the newspaper *Éire Nua – The Irish Nation* on 1 December 1923. It translates as follows:

Denis Barry who had died was OC Republican Police and was also a bosom friend to both Terence MacSwiney and Tomás MacCurtain. He worked with Terence and did so in a manner that earned considerable commendation from Cork Corporation for the work he had done for the peace in the city. When the Free State forces came to Cork they arrested most of the men he had gathered together. He was respected and honoured by all who knew him.

Appendix 5

The roll call of the first meeting of the first Dáil held on 22 January 1919.
(All other elected members were detained in various prisons.)

Dáil Éireann – Volume 1 – 22 January 1919
The Roll of Members was called over by the Clerk and the following teachtaí answered to their names:

Clontarf – R. Mulcahy
College Green – Seán T. O'Kelly
Connemara – P. O'Máille
Cork City – J. J. Walsh
Cork West – Seán O h-Aodha
Donegal North – J. O'Doherty
Donegal South – P. J. Ward
Donegal West – J. Sweeney
Harbour, Dublin – P. Shanahan
Kerry East – P. Beasley

The Unknown Commandant

Kildare North – D. O'Buachalla
Limerick West – C. Ó Coilean
Louth – J. J. O'Kelly
Mayo North – Dr. Crowley
Meath South – E. J. Duggan
Leix – Kevin O'Higgins
Roscommon North – Count Plunkett
Stephen's Green – Alderman Kelly
Tipperary Mid – J. A. Burke
Tipperary South – P. Moloney
Waterford Co – Cathal Brugha
Wexford North – R. Sweetman
Wexford South – Dr. C. Ryan
Wicklow West – R. C. Barton.

Letters and telegrams of congratulation on the Declaration of Independence of the Irish Republic were read.

Mr. T. J. Harbison, teachta for NE Tyrone, wrote acknowledging invitation to attend the Dáil, which invitation he stated he should decline for obvious reasons. He expressed his entire sympathy with the demand of Ireland for a hearing of her just cause at the Congress of the Nations. The contents of the letter were ordered to be published.

Appendix 6

Máire MacSwiney's letter to prisoners, 8 November 1923

'Collapse of Hunger Strike'

Comrades,

Some foolish people are talking about the 'collapse of the hunger-strike and a few have been silly enough to say harsh words to some of those who broke. And so, to all of you – to those I know and to those I don't know – I want to send a greeting and a word of encouragement. I know something about hunger-striking both from trying it myself – and from what is much harder – watching one I loved endure it to death. You will therefore I know pay more attention to what I say than to those who speak in ignorance.

First, the hunger strike has not collapsed, even though the great majority have ceased. That was bound to happen for several reasons; the first being the fact that very very few men can stand starvation – deliberately endure it when food is in sight. Another reason is that the great majority who undertook the hunger strike did it in sympathy with the men in Mountjoy and under the impression that it would be only a matter of a few days. If you are really going to succeed in a hunger-strike you can only do so (1) by having some great motive and (2) by taking it for granted that you are going to die, or at least that there is a good likelihood of it. A sympathetic hunger-strike will not succeed, simply because 'self-preservation is the first law of nature'.

Those who know most about it are the least surprised that the majority have already stopped.

There are three different classes of you, comrades, to whom I want to say a word separately: -

1. Those who broke first from sheer hunger and because they couldn't stick it any longer.
2. Those who came off strike reluctantly and in obedience to orders, in order to preserve or restore discipline in the camps; and
3. Those who are still on, and mean to continue to 'Victory or the grave'.

I have not much to say to those last. They have only to go with me in spirit to Brixton and by that bed-side they may hear me tell them they are one and all my brothers, and that I pray for them and think of them hourly that they may have the strength and endurance to the end, but that the end for them will, I am confident, be Victory with Freedom.

One thing more I would like to say. I am fully sensible that your suffering is greater – and for that reason cannot last so long – because you have not the comfortable bed, warm clothing, fire and careful attention which made the physical suffering easier, nor have you the consolation of relatives constantly with you. God grant you a speedy release.

To you who obeyed probably the hardest order you ever got in your life – hardest to your noble spirits at least whatever the relief to the body, – and who reluctantly abandoned the hunger-strike for the sake of the weaker ones; the most understanding sympathy is due. It is you who are suffering most, whose hearts are almost broken. Won't it help you a little to know that we who understand most have no blame for you. Will you not try to complete your sacrifice by cheering up, and not spoil it by getting bitter. For you may be inclined to get bitter both ways; against those whose failure called you off and against those who when ordered refused to come off.

And without discussing your right to feel bitter, or to get discouraged, I want to plead with you to make up your minds not to do either. You will get your chance yet to do something big for Ireland and you will prove yourselves. The more sure you are of your own ability to have gone on to the end, the more easily you will realise the truth of what I say.

I could name several men I know myself and many more I only know by reputation, who have obeyed orders in this matter, whose courage I would not doubt than I would my brother's. Some people, ever your friends, in the first shock of surprise were disappointed, but not when they understood. If the Government, Army H.Q. and people like myself who have some knowledge of what is

The Unknown Commandant

necessary for organisation and discipline, all agree that you did right, you may be sure the country will accept your verdict. No one who knows me will give me any patience with cowards or slackers. I have not. But then you are neither the one nor the other. I am proud to call you all my friends and I feel sure you will do the big thing now and help in the organisation of the camps cheerfully, patiently and with no grudge of any kind against anybody. Ireland wants us all, those who have limitations and as well as those who have not.

And now for the poor boys who may be feeling a bit downhearted because they broke away under the stress of hunger. Some of you perhaps declare you don't care, you could not stick it; and some others of you are feeling sore and ashamed and sorry you did not try harder. Never mind! You all did your best and if you were not able to fight against the pangs of hunger as well as you fought against the enemies of the Republic remember we are not all asked to do the same kind of work for Ireland. I can do a hunger-strike but I would be a poor hand in a fight, and if I had to do a forced march you would beat me to fits in five minutes. Don't be afraid that you will ever be reproached with a breach of discipline. There is only one kind of discipline that hunger will obey and that is self-discipline and self-control. If you are disappointed with yourselves, work all the harder now; acquire self-discipline; study to make yourselves fit to serve Ireland. I have heard the cheering message sent to you by the O/C. That will cheer you up above all. And if some foolish people do not understand at first what a terrible thing hunger is, well, don't get discouraged. Ireland has plenty work for us all. If you don't do one kind you can do another. No torture inflicted from outside must ever make you give up this Republic. And I am sure it never will.

Cheer up now. Get into good working order again at once. If you are released join your Sinn Féin club. And work for the Local Elections and work hard; if you are not released, yet go ahead inside to make yourselves better citizens of the Republic. And if you don't know Irish study that first. If you do know it teach it to those who don't and talk nothing else.

Beannacht Dé oraibh go léir

Mary MacSwiney

Appendix 7

Messages of sympathy and tributes received by the Barry family on the occasion of the death of Commandant Denis Barry:

- Pádraig Ó Ruitléis, Acting President of the Government of the Republic
- William Hegarty, Town Clerk, Cork
- Blackrock Hurling Club
- National Athletic Association
- Carrigtwohill Sinn Féin Club
- Report of meeting in Riverstick of the Community
- Report of meeting of Cork Corporation
- Report of meeting of Cork County Board of the GAA
- Report of meeting of the Cork Workers' Council

The Unknown Commandant

Sinn Féin
Oifig an Uachtaráin
Baile Átha Cliath
November 20th 1923

To B Barry

A chara

By the death of your brother Ireland has suffered a twofold loss. In his lifetime he had given evidence of a sense of civic responsibility to an extent which evoked the admiration of all who came in contact with him, and with it he combined that purity of motive and unselfishness of purpose which has ever characterised the outstanding figures in the National struggle. In him Ireland has lost a great citizen and a great patriot.

It is a fitting coincidence that he who collaborated so tirelessly and so fearlessly with Terence MacSwiney in the most difficult period of his life's work, should show a like determination and fidelity in upholding their common ideals unto death. It is a tragic commentary on the present phase of the Imperial ruthlessness that he who looked especially to Terence MacSwiney for inspiration and guidance should be the first victim in opposing it.

Your brother's death will bring home to the world the appalling condition in which British diplomacy has reduced our country. It will also bring home to our people the immediate conditions which made the death of such a man possible. His tragic end after fourteen months captivity, without hope of release save at the price of his honour, should bring the blush of shame to the cheeks of those who, by apathy and indifference, share with his executors the responsibility for his death.

Your brother lived and died upholding the honour of his country. Comrades equally inspired and equally true are on the verge of the grave. If forsaken Nationality decrees that they too, should die, his death will be a rallying point in the growing enlightenment of the Nation, which will yet exact a reckoning for the evils wrought in its name.

On behalf of the Nation and of the Cabinet and Government of the Republic, I tender you our proud sympathy. With you we mourn the loss of a sterling citizen and fearless soldier of the Republic.

Mise, do chara
PADRAIG O'RUITLEIS
Acting President
Oifig Clérig na Cathrach
Corcaigh

*

William Hegarty, Town Clerk
Town Clerk's Office
28th November 1923

Dear Madam
At the last Ordinary Meeting of the County Borough Council sympathetic references were made to the death of your son, Denis, and well-merited tributes were paid to his worth as an Irishman and a citizen, and to the

creditable work performed by him as Chief Officer of Police in the City during the troubled times.

The Council have instructed me to convey to you and your family a very sincere expression of their sympathy at the sad event, and adjourned the meeting as a tribute of respect to his memory.

In conveying it I would dearly like to be associated with this expression as an old friend of his for whom I had the greatest possible regard.

Yours faithfully
Liam Ó hÉigeartaigh

*

Blackrock Hurling Club

At a specially convened meeting of the above club, Mr M. Dorney in the chair, the following resolution was proposed by Mr S. Murphy seconded by Mr E. O'Connell: 'That we tender to the relatives of the late Mr. Denis Barry our deepest sympathy in their bereavement'.

The Chairman put the resolution to the meeting, which was passed in silence. The business of the meeting was adjourned as a mark of respect to his memory.

*

National Athletic Association

At the weekly meeting of the Cork County Board of the National Athletic Association, Mr. Fred Harkins presiding, Mr. D. Falvey, Hon. Sec., referred to the death

Appendix 7

Mr. Denis Barry who had been a prominent athlete and at one time representative for Cork on the Governing Council. The duty devolved on him to propose that the sympathy of the Association be passed to his relatives and that they adjourn as a mark of respect.

Mr. T. Hickey seconded. It was only right that they should respect the memory of such a strong athletic advocate.

Other members having joined in the expression of sympathy.

The Chairman in passing the motion, recalled that the late Denis Barry had been his predecessor on the Athletic Council of the Gaelic Association when that body controlled Irish Athletics and few of the competitors of the present day knew of his work for Irish Athletic fixtures. They all deplore his loss. He declared the meeting adjourned.

*

Late Mr D Barry
Carrigtwohill S F Club
At the weekly meeting the following resolution was proposed by Mr. F Deney and seconded by Mr. Thomas Gee, Hon Sec – 'That we adjourn this meeting as a mark of respect to the memory of Commandant D Barry, and that we tender to his relatives our deepest sympathy in their sad bereavement'. Messrs Fitzgerald, M Finn, T O'Brien, J Kelleher etc associated themselves with this motion.
(*Cork Examiner*, 30 November 1923)

*

The Unknown Commandant

Meeting of Sinn Féin Cumann at Riverstick

At a meeting held at Riverstick on the motion of Mr. A Cronin DC, Mr. John Harrington was moved to the chair.

The Chairman said it was with feelings of deep regret that he had to refer to the death of Mr. Denis Barry and explained at some length the idea of his policy. He was forced to say that he carried out his principle, and died for what he fought for. He [chairman] was not a believer in that policy, as he believed in constitutional methods, but he would be wanting in his duty if he did not attend that meeting to pay a deserving tribute to the memory of Mr. Denis Barry as he was one of the best and bravest hurlers in any field in South Cork.

On the motion of Mr. A Cronin, seconded by Mr. Tim Daly, a vote of sympathy was passed to Mr. Barry's family in their sad bereavement.

The motion was put to the meeting and carried in silence.

Members of the Sinn Féin Club were present in large numbers and appealed to the meeting to observe the day of his funeral as a general holiday for the joint parishes of Ballymartle and Belgooly and same was unanimously approved of, the whole parish to attend the funeral.

The Rosary was recited for the repose of his soul.
(*Cork Examiner*, 30 November 1923)

*

Adjournment of Corporation

At a meeting of the Cork Corporation last night, Councillor D Horgan presiding. Mr. Barry said that since their last meeting a citizen had passed away in the person of Mr. D Barry whose death took place in the internment camp. The late Mr. Barry was a worthy citizen, a great soldier and a great Irishman, who, when needed was amongst the most effective to keep the peace in the city. He thought that the treatment handed out to Mr. Barry in prison was such that they would not expect it from any other nation but their own. Mr. Barry had passed away, and he [the speaker] hoped he was in a better place at the present time. He thought the least respect they should show his memory was to adjourn that meeting and send a vote of sympathy to his relatives. He was a great man while the protection of the city was under his hands, although they may be called murderers, robbers and looters. He was sure it was the wish of the Council that they should adjourn.

Mr. Hennessey, as one who knew Mr. Barry for a great many years, seconded the proposition. During the last 10 or 15 years Mr. Barry had rendered services to his country in every way without ever expecting to be rewarded. Everyone remembered the troubled times of 1920 and 1921 and during that period he personally could testify to the fact that Mr. Barry never went to bed until 3 and 4 o'clock in the morning because his duty compelled him to walk the streets and keep the city free from crime. He thought they should also adjourn as a protest against the conditions under which he was held in the internment camps.

Mr. Kelleher HC, in joining in the expression of regret, said that the constitutional way was, from first to last, the best. He deeply sympathised with Mr. Barry's relatives in their bereavement.

The Unknown Commandant

Ald. E Coughlan said he knew Denis Barry during the troubled times and he did very valuable work in keeping the peace of the city. He thought the Government should take Cardinal Logue's advice and let the prisoners out.

The Chairman said he hoped no member would think that he raised this for the purpose of Republican propaganda. He believed the Treaty should be worked, and he also thought that the Republicans should be allowed to work now on constitutional lines. They all hoped that no more Irishmen would pass away as the result of the hunger-strike.

(*Cork Examiner*, 30 November 1923)

*

Action of Cork County Board

Mr. W. P. Aherne presided and there also attended Messrs P. O'Keeffe, Secretary; A. Fitzgerald, Bride Valley; C. O'Mahony, Nils, J. O'Callaghan, Charleville; J. J. Buckley, Mallow; P. Clifford, St Mary's; J. J. Sexton, Cloghduv; J. Harrington, Aughabullogue; J. Dennehy, UCC; C. O'Donovan, UCC; J. Collins, Youghal; D. Hartnett, Castle Treasure; F. Kelleher, Shamrocks; J. O'Donovan, Father Mathew Hall; F. McElligott, Evergreen; P. J. Long, Kilmurry; S. O'Hegarty, Glen Rovers; P. Sexton, Owenabue; P. Keane, Lees; P. J. O'Sullivan, Inniscarra; D. O'Kelly, Glenview, M. H. Murphy, E. Fleming, M. McGrath, Sarsfields.

The Chairman said that since their last meeting an ex-member of the Board and a prominent hurler and footballer who had assisted the county in many important contests had passed away. He was sure they all regretted the sad death of Mr. Denis Barry, and he asked the members whether having passed a vote of sympathy with the late Mr. Barry's relatives they would adjourn the Board as a mark of respect to Mr. Barry's memory.

Mr. J. J. Sexton then proposed a vote of condolence and the adjournment of the Board. It was the least tribute they could pay to one who was a colleague of theirs and a member of the Blackrock Hurling Club.

Mr. James Harrington in seconding the motion said the late Mr. Barry was a parishioner of his. He was a brilliant hurler as well as an athlete, and he was certain they all deplored his death under such sad circumstances.

Mr. Long associated himself with the vote of sympathy and said that it was their duty to adjourn out of respect to his memory. He was a good Gael and a good Irish man.

Mr. A. Fitzgerald, in supporting the motion, said that he had played with the late Mr. Barry and had always found him a true and honest Gael. He was sorry that the occasion had arisen for the motion.

Mr. Keane also joined in the tribute to the late Mr. Barry, as did Thomas Dooley.

Mr. Fleming, Midleton, said he wished to be associated with the expression of regret. They, as Gaels, deeply deplored Mr. Barry's death. The late Mr. Barry was highly esteemed and respected by every member of the association, and by his countrymen in general. Mr. Barry had made the supreme sacrifice and he was sure his loss would be felt not alone by the members of the Gaelic Athletic Association, but by all Irishmen. They appreciated his services as a Gael and an Irishman.

The Unknown Commandant

The other members also joined in the vote of condolence. In declaring the vote of sympathy passed and the adjournment of the Board, the chairman inquired what action the board would take concerning the fixtures for Sunday. Mr. C O'Donovan proposed that all fixtures for Sunday to be put off. Mr. James Harrington seconded. Mr. Clifford said, that while he deeply regretted the death of Mr. Barry, he thought the matches should go on. Mr. McElligott seconded, and on a show of hands the amendment was defeated by 13 to 3 votes.

All matches were accordingly declared off for Sunday.

(*Cork Examiner*, 21 November 1923)

*

Cork Worker's Council
Late Mr. Denis Barry
Harbour Board Employees

Mr. G Nason (President) occupied the chair and representatives from the affiliated bodies were in attendance. The President referred to the death of Mr. Denis Barry and said up to a short time ago he was a worker and he was also a man who endeared himself to a good many people of the city, especially during the Black and Tan times when he filled the position of Chief Commissioner of Police in Cork. Members of the Council met him on many occasions on labour questions and also on charitable matters, and he never showed the cold shoulder to them. Mr. Barry was to his opinions, the same as any other members of his community. Everyone, including those who differed from Mr. Barry's opinions, however, abjured the action that had been taken in depriving Mr. Barry's relatives of his body. The Irish people had always respect for their dead, and the fact that those who were nearest and dearest to Mr. Barry had been deprived of his body was a matter of great comment amongst all classes in the city. They had always denounced harsh acts, and they would continue to do so. He suggested that they should pass a vote of condolence to the deceased relatives in their great bereavement, express their indignation at the action of keeping the deceased's body from his relatives and adjourn their meeting as a mark of respect to the deceased's memory.

Mr. J Hickey said everyone felt sore at the detention of Mr. Barry's body, after Mr. Barry had been kept in prison without trial and left to die on hunger strike. He did not think any purpose could be served by passing a vote of sympathy or condolence. They should take action against the Government that kept Mr. Barry in prison without preferring a charge against him, or putting him on trial and that detained his body from his relatives who wished to bury him in consecrated ground. He therefore moved that the meeting be adjourned as a protest against the action of the Government in detaining the body of Mr. Barry from his relatives and family.

Mr. A Daly seconded the motion.

Mr. A J Kelleher, TC, HC, said he agreed with the protest regarding the withholding of the deceased's body from his relatives and he also agreed that the deceased's family and relations deserved their sympathy and condolences for their bereavement, but he disagreed on the question of the adjournment of the meeting. That Council should not be used as a political stepladder for any political party. He moved as an amendment that the Council should offer its deep sympathy to the relatives, and protest against the action of keeping the body from the family and relatives.

Mr. R Anthony seconded. While they deeply sympathised with the relatives in their bereavement there was always a danger in matters of that kind of trying to make the Council take sides with one or other of the big political parties in the country. They should take advantage of the lessons they had learned in the past. That Council had too often been used for the purposes of basing an attack on the Government or some outside party. He disagreed with such a policy and on more than one occasion he had registered his protest against it. He did not want to refer to the question of delivering an opinion on the mortality of a hunger-strike. He would leave that to those whose calling and education fitted them to be a guide.

(*Cork Examiner*, 24 November 1923)

Appendix 8

Éire Nua – The Irish Nation, Saturday 2 December 1923

The Testimony of Denis Barry

We were among gentle enemies when the news came of Denis Barry's death, and there was bewilderment on them and dismay. 'Where is the logic of it?' they asked unhappily. 'A man hunger-strikes for his release and dies! Surely even prison is better than that death. Is it not insane pride? How can his dying serve any cause?' and for us, the logic of it was so overwhelming, the sense of how he had served his cause so poignant that when we should have answered we were dumb. It is after a while only that praise and pity began to unravel themselves in thought. Very simple, the logic of it is. No prisoner hunger-strikes to the death of his own pride's sake; his hunger strike, from the first moment to the last breath, is a declaration of his faith – his faith that the cause he upholds is just and holy and that those who imprison him for upholding it have no rightful authority in the land.

The Unknown Commandant

There is a tragedy more pitiful than physical death; the tragedy of kindly men and women, lovers of their country, who in mere blindness ally themselves with the forces of tyranny and untruth. That alliance once made only the evil thrives and darkness envelops the whole spirit until conscience, honour and kindliness are dead.

The hunger striker knows that the slow degradation of human beings, the slow corruption of a nation, may continue unheeded for long years while the iron hand is hidden in a velvet glove and oppression wears a cloak of lies. He resolves as all challengers of hypocrisy have resolved: if only by suffering its worst fury on his own body to force the evil thing to unmask. He knows that the tyranny which leaves men and women to rot in jail slowly may be tolerated for a long time by a people drugged into apathy with lies; it is only when the prisoners choose to die rather than endure it that this tyranny stands revealed for what it is. It is a mortal combat the hunger striker is waging against oppression and ignorance and untruth.

His whole fight is a spiritual one; he wars against no human being, only against darkness in men's hearts; he uses no weapon to harm any man; he endures all, inflicts nothing. It is a battle in which he alone is sacrificed and his enemies receive no wound. His sole trust is in the justice of his cause and the secret knowledge of its justice which is hidden, however timidly, in the people's hearts. Maybe his ordeal will call that secret knowledge out bravely into the open day in time to save his life; maybe it is only his death that will awaken it; living or dying, he believes that his work will be done. The logic of his sacrifices is this.

Appendix 8

'Men have died' Pádraic Pearse wrote in *The Singer*, 'for worthless causes, for foolish causes, for wicked causes', but has it been known in the world's history that a man or woman, for a worthless cause, died on hunger-strike in jail?

It is a slow, unnatural, creeping death, the suffering increases, remorselessly, every hour; all vitality ebbs out of the body, leaving only one vision clear, and the spirit is choosing afresh at every moment, all those nights and days, between the salvation the body craves for and faithfulness to that vision in the mind. If that ideal were false, unreal, an illusion, would it not crumble and vanish in thirty nights and days? Would not the natural energies that please on the side of life find a thousand reasons why the man should not die? Would mere pride sustain that long controversy that mortal tests? Would any faith sustain it that any argument could prove untrue? Men have died for unworthy causes, fighting for them out of some thoughtless loyalty, at best, to country or lord or clan – but not that death.

Ghouls Shrink from Funeral
Denis Barry's and Andrew Sullivan's Victory in Death

The decision of the Free State Government not to hand over the body of Denis Barry to his relatives is the most striking proof which could be afforded of the state of abject terror in which they find themselves. It is a confession that they are conscious of the extent to which they have outraged the public conscience by the course they have adopted towards the hunger strikers. They know that, morally, they are just as responsible for the deaths of Denis Barry and Andrew Sullivan and any other of their comrades in suffering and heroism whom the angel of death may yet summon to their Great Account, as if they had taken them out and shot them against the wall as they did Rory O'Connor and Liam Mellows.

They meant to keep them in prison for an indefinite period without charge or trial. They instructed their underlings to treat them as common criminals in order to break their spirit and degrade them in their own eyes. They caused ill usage, hardships and indignities to be inflicted on them in various ways, until at last the prisoners felt that anything was better than to continue to be the victims of such treatment. It was only because of the systematic policy set afoot by the Free State Government that the hunger strike was resorted to. That was felt to be the only alternative to a condition of things which self-respecting men could no longer endure. The treatment of the prisoners aroused among the public feelings of passionate indignation such as have rarely been witnessed. From nine-tenths of the public boards come insistent demands that their torture should cease and that their prison doors should be thrown open. Free State Ministers snapped their fingers at all requests of this kind. They were indifferent to human suffering. They did not care whether or not the prisoners died. Their plea was that the safety of their ramshackle Free State was their only consideration.

At last Cardinal Logue found it necessary to intervene. He knew that there could be no justification for condemning to what amounted to perpetual imprisonment people who had broken no law and against

Appendix 8

whom no charge could or would be made. But even then the Free State Government was obdurate. They could not afford to listen to the appeal of charity even though voiced by the Cardinal Primate.

It was then that Denis Barry, after thirty-four days of the agony which a hunger-strike must involve, died. His death immediately brought matters to a head. If his body were delivered to his relatives, Free State Ministers know that there would be a funeral from Dublin to Cork which, in its character and dimensions, would recall that of Terence Bellew MacManus in Fenian times.

In that demonstration they would see their condemnation and their doom. No one could then be in any doubt as to the feelings entertained for the Free State Government. In order to afford no opportunity for such an expression of opinion they decided not to give up the body, but to inter it themselves in the precincts of the prison camp. Such a course is, of course, as illegal as it is inhuman. They have no power to retain the remains of an untried prisoner. Their law, such as it is, would compel them to refrain from treating the lifeless corpse as they had treated its Creator and Judge, their authority over the body ceased.

Probably, after coming to their decision, they discovered that this was the case. Other men were, also, on the point of death, and they should have to play the part of ghoul to their bodies when they, too, died. Meanwhile, the public were looking on, horrified and amazed, at the sort of thing which masqueraded as a Government in Ireland. Through a thousand channels they learned they had gone too far. There was a violent

The Unknown Commandant

swing of opinion against them, and they were assured that the longer they persisted in their brutal illegality, the more fatal the result would be. It was only, then, in sheer terror, that they entered into negotiations which led to the calling off of the hunger strike on the distinct understanding that there would be a general jail.

It was the death of Denis Barry which was the direct cause of the bringing about this consummation.

Appendix 9

Letter from Military Archives, Cathal Brugha Barracks

In September 2006 when the author began work on this book he sought information from military archives about Denis Barry's internment and death. The following reply was received.

Military Archives
Cathal Brugha Barracks
Rathmines
Dublin 6

01 November 2006
Mr. D. A Barry
Cork

Dear Mr. Barry

Thank you for your letter of 27th September 2006.

The Unknown Commandant

All we have in Military Archives relating to Republican Prisoners are a number of prison ledgers for a number of locations together with a number of boxes of general documentation. The following is an extract from the efforts of an individual who has been working in this area over the last number of years and who has conducted a thorough examination of the material available.

Name: Denis Barry
Address: Cullen, Riverstick, Ballymantel [sic], Kinsale.
Prison No: 10234 (Very similar to the one, i.e. 1014, that you supplied and may be due to a transcription error on either of our parts)
Place of Arrest: Glashaboy North, Currignavara [sic]
Date of arrest: 08 October 1922
Release Date: 06 June 1923. (This would seem to indicate that he was re-arrested subsequently. Why, where and under what circumstances I am unable to state)
Remarks: Brigade Police Officer, Cork No. 1. Charged with the murder of O'Callaghan and Hanlon. Looted O'Connells. (I have been unable to trace the background or date of these charges. The anti Treaty side would probably have used 'commandeered' or 'requisitioned' instead of 'looted'.) Died Curragh Hospital 20 November 1923. (The material in archives does not describe the circumstances of his death.)

I hope that this information will be of assistance to you in compiling a family history.

Yours sincerely
(Signed) Staff Officer

Appendix 9

Author's note

It appears that the writer has confused Denis Barry with another Volunteer named Barry who was released in June 1923. Denis was interned from October 1922 until his death in custody in November 1923. Had he, as the letter suggests, in fact been charged with murder and re-arrested, as happened to others at the time, he would have been court-martialled and executed.

This confusion has led to unwarranted assumptions which demean Denis Barry's memory and calls into question the integrity of record-keeping in the Military Archives. Eight senior army officers attend his inquest in Naas and yet the Military Archives in Cathal Brugha Barracks have no record of this.

Appendix 10

Cork No. 1 Brigade – chronology of engagements 1918–1921

July 8, 1918	First attack on Royal Irish Constabulary at Beal a Ghleanna.
Sept 3, 1918	Successful raid for weapons by Volunteers on Cork Grammar School at Wellington Road.
Nov 11, 1918	Donnachada MacNiallghuis rescued from Cork Jail.
Nov 18, 1919	IRA raid Murray's gun shop at Patrick Street for arms and ammunition.
Jan 3, 1920	Capture of Carrigtwohill RIC Barracks in East Cork.
Jan 30, 1920	Tomás MacCurtain, Officer Commanding Cork No. 1 Brigade, elected Lord Mayor.
Feb 9, 1920	Capture of Castlemartyr RIC Barracks in East Cork.
Feb 17, 1920	IRA attach RIC despatch party near Union Quay, Cork city.
March 1920	Black and Tans arrive in Ireland in Cork city,

	they establish their headquarters at Empress Place, Summerhill.
March 11, 1920	RIC District Inspector McDonagh shot and seriously wounded.
March 11, 1920	RIC member Timothy Scully shot dead at Glanmire.
March 19, 1920	Shooting of RIC Constable Murtagh at Popes Quay, Cork city.
March 20, 1920	Tomás MacCurtain shot dead at his home at Thomas Davis Street.
March 31, 1920	Terence MacSwiney elected Lord Mayor of Cork.
April 5, 1920	Burning of income tax offices at South Mall and South Terrace and Togher RIC barracks in Cork city.
May 8, 1920	Capture of Cloyne RIC Barracks in East Cork.
May 11, 1920	RIC Sergeant Garvey and Constable Harrington shot dead.
May 12, 1920	Burning of Commons Road RIC barracks in Cork city.
June 1, 1920	Blarney RIC barracks attacked by large party of IRA.
June 1, 1920	Ambush of Cameron Regiment near Midleton in East Cork.
June 24, 1920	Blackrock RIC barracks, on outskirts of Cork city, is attacked and set on fire.
July 2, 1920	Military vehicle from Victoria Barracks hijacked at Cork Railway Station
July 12, 1920	Three RIC barracks burned – at King Street, St Lukes and Lower Glanmire Road, Cork city.
July 15, 1920	Two British Army lorries captured and burned at Dennehy's Cross, Cork city.
July 17, 1920	Divisional Commissioner Gerald Bryce-Ferguson Smyth shot dead by the IRA at County Club, South Mall.

Appendix 10

August 4, 1920	British curfew patrol fired upon at Blackpool in Cork city.
August 5, 1920	Curfew patrol again attacked at Blackpool.
August 6, 1920	Ambush of Cameron Highlanders at Whiterock, Midleton.
August 7, 1920	Curfew patrol fired upon at Batchelor's Quay.
August 9, 1920	Cufew patrol fired upon at Cattle Lane.
August 10, 1920	Curfew patrol fired upon at the Colosseum Cinema, MacCurtain Street.
August 11, 1920	Republican prisoners at Cork gaol begin hunger strike.
August 12, 1920	City Hall raided by British army personnel. Terence McSwiney arrested – begins hunger strike.
August 21, 1920	Shooting dead of RIC Sergeant Daniel Maunsell at Inchigeelagh.
August 22, 1920	RIC District Inspector Swanzy shot dead in Lisburn by members of Cork No. 1 Brigade IRA.
Sept, 1920	Full-time city Active Service Unit formed from the 1st and 2nd Battalions, No. 1 Brigade.
Sept 24, 1920	Failed attempted capture of General Strickland at MacCurtain Street.
Oct 3, 1920	Shooting of RIC Constable Chave at Patrick Street, Cork city.
Oct 8, 1920	One British Auxiliary shot dead and another injured in attack in Cork city centre.
Oct 8, 1920	One British soldier killed and three wounded in attack on military lorry at Barrack Street, Cork city.
Oct 25, 1920	Seán O'Hegarty assumes command of Cork No. 1 Brigade IRA.
Oct 25, 1920	Death of Volunteer Joe Murphy on hunger strike at Cork Prison.
Oct 25, 1920	Death of Terence MacSwiney on hunger strike at Brixton Prison.

The Unknown Commandant

Oct 29, 1920	Two Royal Artillery intelligence officers shot dead by IRA near Glenville, north of Cork city.
Nov 16, 1920	Three British army officers shot dead by IRA at Waterfall, on outskirts of Cork city.
Nov 18, 1920	RIC Sergeant J. O'Donoghue shot dead at White Street.
Nov 18, 1920	Three civilians shot dead by Black and Tans at Broad Street, Broad Lane and North Mall in Cork city.
Nov 21, 1920	Week-long spate of bomb and arson attacks by Anti Sinn Féin Society begins in Cork city centre.
Nov 23, 1920	Three members of Cork No. 1 Brigade IRA killed in explosion at Patrick Street, Cork city.
Nov 23, 1920	British Army intelligence officer shot dead by IRA near Ballincollig.
Nov 27, 1920	Volunteer William Heffernan shot dead by British forces at Castlemartyr.
Nov 27, 1920	Parish halls in Cork city at Blackrock and Douglas burned down by Anti Sinn Féin Society.
Nov 30, 1920	Thomas Ashe (Sinn Féin) Club, Morrison's Island, burned down by British sympathisers.
Dec 3, 1920	RIC Constable Maurice Prendeville shot dead at Youghal.
Dec 11, 1920	Daring escape by Volunteers in Cloyne.
Dec 11, 1920	Delany brothers shot dead by British forces at Dublin Hill, Cork city.
Dec 11, 1920	Auxiliaries ambushed at Dillons Cross.
Dec 12, 1920	Burning of Cork city centre and City Hall.
Dec 28, 1920	Offices and machinery of *Cork Examiner* newspaper destroyed.
Dec 29, 1920	Three Black and Tans shot dead and three seriously wounded in IRA attack at Midleton's Main Street.
Dec 29, 1920	Black and Tan reinforcements suffer casualties

Appendix 10

	when ambushed at Mile Bush near Midleton.
Jan 1, 1921	First British 'official' reprisals are carried out in Midleton.
Jan 4, 1921	Parnell Bridge ambush – two RIC members shot dead and five wounded. Five civilians also wounded.
Jan 10, 1921	Constables Carroll and Sheehan of the RIC shot and wounded in IRA attack in Cork city.
Jan 21, 1921	RIC Sergeant Bloxham shot dead and Head Constable Larkin wounded in ambush at Waterfall.
Jan 28, 1921	IRA suffer losses at Dripsey Ambush, ten miles west of Cork city.
Feb, 1921	Separate Cork city command of the IRA formed – Thomas Crofts appointed Officer Commanding.
Feb 2, 1921	Captain Joseph Murphy, No. 2 Brigade IRA, executed at Victoria Barracks, Cork city.
Feb 3, 1921	Three Black and Tans shot dead in ambush at Ballinhassig, about seven miles west of Cork city.
Feb 20, 1921	IRA suffer major losses at Clonmult in East Cork.
Feb 25, 1921	Ambush of Auxiliaries at Coolnacahera (Coolavokig), on the road between Ballyvourney and Macroom.
Feb 28, 1921	Six members of the IRA executed at the military detention barracks in Cork city.
Feb 28, 1921	Series of retaliatory attacks against British forces in Cork city – six soldiers killed and at least six wounded.
Feb 28, 1921	Setback for IRA in foiled Passage West ambush.
March 1, 1921	Charles Daly of C Company, 2nd Battalion, Cork No. 1 Brigade IRA, shot dead.
March 23, 1921	Black and Tans kill six members of Cork No. 1

	Brigade at Clogheen, on the outskirts of Cork city.
April 10, 1921	British troops wounded when landmine explodes under their lorry at Churchtown North, near Midleton.
April 17, 1921	RIC Constable John Cyril MacDonald shot dead at Cove Street, Cork city.
April 19, 1921	Tadhg O'Sullivan of C Company, 2nd Battalion, Cork No. Brigade IRA, shot dead.
April 29, 1921	Dramatic rescue of three IRA officers from Spike Island.
May 8, 1921	RIC Constable Fredrick Sterland shot dead at Cook Street, Cork city.
May 8, 1921	British troops take over Moore's Hotel and Hibernian Hall in Cork city for use as military outposts.
May 8, 1921	Local man Willie Brandsfield shot dead at Carrigtwohill by soldiers from the Cameron Highlanders regiment.
May 14, 1921	Five members of the security forces shot dead by the IRA in Midleton.
May 14, 1921	Three RIC members killed in ambush at Watercourse Road, Cork city.
May 15, 1921	In Carrigtwohill, three men are taken from their homes and shot dead by the Cameron Highlanders.
May 16, 1921	Father James O'Callaghan, curate of the North Cathedral, shot dead at the home of Liam de Roiste TD.
May 23, 1921	Stephen Dorman, E Company, 2nd Battalion, Cork No. 1 Brigade IRA, shot dead at Douglas Street.
May 25, 1921	Houses at Shandon Street and Blackpool burned in retaliation for attacks on Crown forces in Cork city.

Appendix 10

May 28, 1921	Diarmuid O'Hurley, East Cork battalion column leader, shot dead by Black and Tans.
May 31, 1921	Bomb attack on band members of 2nd Hampshire regiment at Youghal – seven killed and ten wounded.
June 24, 1921	RIC barracks at Tuckey Street, Shandon Street and Douglas burned in Cork city.
June 27, 1921	IRA Commandant Leo Murphy shot dead by Black and Tans at Waterfall, a few miles west of Cork city.
July 3, 1921	British forces suffer a number of casualties in landmine explosion at Carrigshane Cross near Midleton.
July 7, 1921	RIC member shot dead at Ballinhassig.
July 8, 1921	Denis Spriggs shot dead at Blarney Road, Cork city.
July 10, 1921	Four British soldiers shot dead at the Lough, Cork city.

Cumann na mBan insignia (Barry family archive)

Appendix 11

A Tribute to Brave Women

Cumann na mBan held its first meeting in Wynn's Hotel, Dublin, in April 1914. They held their first meeting in Cork in the City Hall in June 1914. This was a well-attended meeting. Within four years a total of eighteen branches were affiliated to the Cork District Council. One of the issues taken on by Cumann na mBan was a campaign to give women the right to vote, which they did not have at that time. The activities of Cumann na mBan embraced the collection of intelligence data by, for example, placing members in employment in offices in the British military establishment; the carrying of despatches; the nursing in secret of wounded Republicans; the collection of funds; the provision of food, clothing, tobacco and other necessities for men on the run. The national organiser for Cumann na mBan was Miss Leslie Price, later to marry General Tom Barry and become President of the Irish Red Cross Organisation.

The Unknown Commandant

By the middle of 1920 the women were fully organised in Cork, and, led by its Presidents Maeve and Nan Hegarty, was of vital help to the Volunteers. They complemented and supported the men in the battle. Some of the women were trained in making bombs and one of its active members, Mary Ellen Hegarty (née Moore), sister of Seán Ó Mórdha, who was secretary of the Cork Comhairle of Sinn Féin, received serious burn injuries to her arms, face, and side. She resumed duty after a painful recovery period. More recently, papers have become to hand, showing how some of the political leaders at the time felt about the organisation and its leaders. The work carried out by them was largely forgotten until 2006, when the Cork City Council created a new walkway in the Mardyke area of the city. A plaque honouring Cumann na mBan was unveiled by the Lord Mayor of Cork, Councillor Deirdre Clune and, fittingly, an honour party of eight female officers of Óglaigh na hÉireann paid full military honours to all of the women who had served their country during the War of Independence.

On the other hand the Government of the day had different views. In a letter from W. T. Cosgrave dated 18 November 1922 to his friend, Rev. Edward J. Byrne, Archbishop of Dublin, we learn of his attitude to Cumann na mBan to whom he referred as 'women revolutionaries'. When the Archbishop appealed to Cosgrave on behalf of hunger striker Máire MacSwiney (sister of Terence MacSwiney) he got a firm slap on the wrist and a lecture about the destructive role of the women in the Civil War.

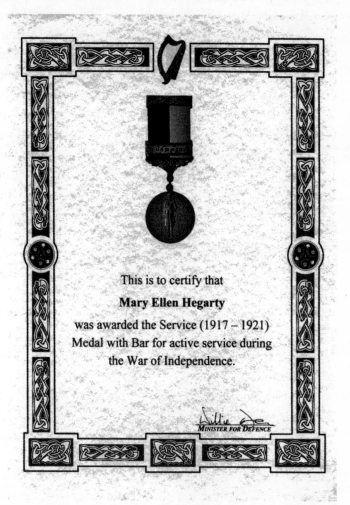

This is to certify that

Mary Ellen Hegarty

was awarded the Service (1917 – 1921)
Medal with Bar for active service during
the War of Independence.

MINISTER FOR DEFENCE

Service certificate of Mary Ellen Hegarty (Barry family archive)

The Unknown Commandant

'Your Grace, you may not be wholly cognisant of the pre-eminent and destructive part played by women in the present deplorable revolt against the definitely express will of the vast majority of the Irish people, and against these sacred principles upon which civilisation and even Christianity itself is founded.'

Presumably Cosgrave was here referring to the general election of June 1922 where the pro-treaty faction, headed by himself, won a majority. Women had only partial voting rights from 1918. Additional rights were granted in 1928. Perhaps Cosgrave should have said 'the vast majority of the male population who voted' so as to validate his comments to his friend the Archbishop.

Mary Ellen Hegarty, mother of the author's wife, was a sister of Seán Ó Mórdha referred to in a previous chapter. She was better known as 'Sis' Moore. She was active in Cumann na mBan from 1917 until March 1923 according

to her Military Service Certificate. Her other brother was Dan Moore who also was a teacher in the North Monastery. He was a founder member with Jack Lynch and Dr Saunders MOH of St Anne's Adoption Society. The author has been unable to establish if he participated in the War of Independence.

Mary Ellen Hegarty (Barry family archive)

Appendix 12

Fr Albert Biddy and Fr Dominc O'Connor

No Roll of Honour would be complete without the names of Fr Albert Biddy and Fr Dominic O'Connor, both Franciscan Capuchin priests. These two men were personally involved in ministering to the men and women patriots of the 1916 Rising and later during the Civil War and in the post-hunger-strike period gave succour to the families of men to whom the official Catholic Church had denied the last rites. In the early 1920s they were effectively exiled to the American Missions in response to complaints from Bishop Cohalan of Cork and the government of the day. Fr Albert died within a few months and Fr Dominic in 1958. In the same year, thanks to the efforts of President Seán T. O'Kelly, An Taoiseach Éamon de Valera, Seán O'Hegarty and the Provincial of the Capuchin Order, their bodies were returned to Ireland and after full religious and civil ceremonies, were laid to rest in the Capuchin Cemetery in Rochestown, Cork.

The Unknown Commandant

Many other priests tended to the spiritual needs of those involved in the 'Troubles'. In particular, mention must be made of the Dominicans for their services in Newbridge and the Curragh. It is also remarkable that in defiance of Bishop Cohalan's edict some of the priests of his diocese rendered spiritual comfort to many of 'The Boys from County Cork'.

Biographical Notes

Brugha, Cathal (1874–1922)
Born in 1874. As a young man Cathal joined the Volunteers and Conradh na Gaelige. Wounded during the 1916 Rising, he became Chief of Staff of the IRA after his release from jail in 1917. Elected TD for Waterford in 1918, he presided at the first meeting of Dáil Éireann in 1919. He was shot and killed by the forces of the National Army in the first days of the Civil War.

Cohalan, Bishop Daniel (1858–1952)
Born 14 July 1858, Kilmichael, County Cork. Ordained in 1882, he was appointed Bishop of Cork in 1916, a position he held until his death in 1952.

Collins, Michael (1890–1922)
'The Big Fellow' was born in 1890 near Clonakilty, County Cork. It is difficult to capture in a short biographical note how any man could pack in so much work into thirty-two short years. He was involved with the GAA, IRB, IRA and Sinn Féin. He fought in the GPO garrison in 1916. He was appointed Minister for Home Affairs and later to the Finance portfolio after the Sinn Féin victory in the 1918 election. He was also Director of Organisation

and Intelligence for the Volunteers. He was joint leader with Arthur Griffith of the Irish delegation at the treaty negotiations. He was Commander-in-Chief of the Free State Army at the outbreak of the Civil War.

He was shot dead in an ambush in August 1922 at Béal na mBláth by a fellow Irishman.

Cosgrave, W. T. (1880–1965)

Cosgrave took part in the Easter Rising 1916, was arrested and sentenced to death. Later he was reprieved and shipped to Frongoch Internment Camp and detained there until 1917. With Denis Barry as his election agent he won a by-election in Kilkenny in 1917. Re-elected in 1918, he held many positions in Government. He was President of the Executive Council of the Irish Free State from 1922 to 1932. He retired from politics in 1945. He was reported as stating in October 1923 during the hunger strike by his former comrades that they could all die before he would interfere for their welfare. (Dáil Reports)

Delany, Con (1891–1920) & Jeremiah (1886–1920)

The Delany brothers were very active in the Volunteer movement. Their house and farm at Dublin Hill just beyond Blackpool in Cork was often used as a safe storage area for the limited arsenal that the Volunteers had at that time. On the night of the burning of Cork city a party of armed men raided their house. They went to the bedroom where Con and Jerry were and shot them both there. Jerry died immediately and Con survived almost a week. They are both buried in the Republican Plot in St Finbarr's Cemetery in Cork.

Johnson, Thomas (1872–1963)

Thomas Johnson was an Irish nationalist and Labour Party leader. He led the Irish Labour Party in the United Kingdom parliament.

Biographical Notes

Later, after Irish independence, he was elected TD for Dublin County to the first Dáil in the 1922 and was the leader of the Labour Party until 1927. As such, he was Leader of the Opposition in the Dáil of the Irish Free State, as Sinn Féin refused to recognise the Dáil as constituted. He is the only Leader of the Opposition to have come from the Labour Party, or indeed from any party other than Fianna Fáil or Fine Gael. He lost his Dáil seat at the September 1927 general election, and the following year was elected to Seanad Éireann, where he served until its abolition in 1936.

Lynch, Liam (1893–1923)

Liam Lynch was born in County Limerick in 1893. A member of the Supreme Council of the IRB he was Divisional Commandant in 1921. He was totally opposed to the Treaty. He became Chief of Staff of the anti-treaty wing of the IRA. He was involved in a skirmish in the Knockmealdown Mountains with the Free State army, and was shot and died on 10 April 1923. He is buried in Kilcrumper Cemetery near Fermoy in County Cork. His remains lie next to his comrade Michael Fitzgerald who died on hunger strike on 17 October 1920.

MacCurtain, Tomás (1884–1920)

Born in Ballyknockane, County Cork, in 1884, he came to Cork city thirteen years later. He became a full-time teacher and organiser for Conradh na Gaelige. He was one of the Organisers of the first meeting of the Volunteers in Cork. After the 1916 Rising he was arrested and held at Frongoch, Wakefield and Reading jails. He was Commandant of the Cork No. 1 Brigade. On 30 January 1920 he was elected Lord Mayor of Cork. He was brutally murdered by British and RIC officers in his home in Blackpool, Cork on 19 March 1920.

The Unknown Commandant

MacNeill, Eoin (1867–1954)

Born in Glenarm in County Antrim, he became Chief of Staff of the Volunteers. He issued the order to call off the Easter Rising. He was arrested, but released in 1917. He was a member of the Sinn Féin executive and was elected to Dáil Éireann. He was appointed Minister for Industry and Commerce in April 1919. He died in 1945.

MacSwiney, Máire (1872–1942)

Born in Cork city in 1872, Máire, a sister of Terence, was a true Republican. She was a leading member of Cumann na mBan and was elected as a Sinn Féin TD. She gave the oration at the funeral of Commandant Denis Barry and she had a major public dispute with Bishop Cohalan of Cork regarding the Bishop's refusal to allow Denis Barry's remains to be received into any Catholic church in the Cork diocese. She pursued his decree of excommunication, assisted by Seán O'Hegarty, for many years, including sending letters to the Pope in Rome. She and her sister Áine established a private school in Cork.

MacSwiney, Terence (1879–1920)

Born in Cork city in 1879, Terence MacSwiney was a teacher and an intellectual. A leading member of the Volunteers, he was second in command to Tomás MacCurtain. He was arrested after the 1916 Rising and detained in Frongoch Internment Camp and Reading Jail. He was released in 1917. He was elected TD for Mid-Cork and Deputy Lord Mayor of Cork in January 1920. He became Lord Mayor in March 1920 following the murder of Tomás MacCurtain. Arrested at Cork City Hall in August 1920 he was sentenced to two years' imprisonment for possession of an alleged incriminating document. He died after a hunger strike lasting seventy-four days on 25 October 1920. He is buried in the Republican Plot in St Finbarr's Cemetery Cork.

Biographical Notes

Maguire, Conor (1889–1971)

Born in Cong, County Mayo, Conor Maguire was educated at Clongowes Wood College and the National University of Ireland. He qualified as a solicitor in 1914 and transferred to the Bar in 1922. He acted as a judge of the provisional Dáil Courts from 1920–1922, and as a Settlement Land Commissioner for Dáil Éireann. He was called to the Inner Bar in 1932 and was a senator for the National University of Ireland from 1932–1936, serving as Attorney General in the first Fianna Fáil administration during that time. He was appointed a judge of the High Court in 1936 and became Chief Justice in 1946.

Mulcahy, Richard (1886–1971)

Richard Mulcahy was Minister for Defence in the Free State Government that refused to release the body of Denis Barry after his death. Born in Waterford in 1886, he joined the Volunteers in 1913, was arrested after the Easter Rising and interned at Frongoch. He was released under the general amnesty in 1917. Pro-treaty, he was Minister for Defence from 1923 to 1924 and leader of Fine Gael from 1944 to 1959.

Murphy, Seán Óg (1897–1956)

Born the son of a Republican in Merchant Street in Cork city before moving with his family to Sundays Well, Seán Óg Murphy learned his hurling skills at the North Monastery School. He played with the Blackrock and the Cork County teams. In 1912 his name appears as a substitute on the Cork team. He won five County Championship medals with Blackrock and three All-Ireland Hurling medals with Cork. Owing to a serious shoulder injury he was forced to retire from playing in 1929. He then gave thirty years of service to the Cork County Board as an administrator. He died suddenly in 1956. He is remembered by the GAA by the Seán Óg Murphy Cup, which is awarded to winners of the Cork County Senior Hurling Championship.

Murphy, Timothy J. (died 29 April 1949)

A senior Irish Labour Party politician, he was first elected to Dáil Éireann at the 1923 general election as a TD for Cork West. He was re-elected at the next nine general elections, but remained on the opposition benches of the Dáil until 1948 when the Labour Party joined the First Inter-Party Government. The Taoiseach, John A. Costello, then appointed him Minister for Local Government.

O'Connor, Rory (1883–1922)/Mellows, Liam (1895–1922)/Barrett, Dick (1899–1922)/McKelvey, Joe (died 1922)

Executed by a 'Free State' firing squad in a revenge killing for the shooting of Seán Hales TD, these men were selected for execution because they were prominent Republicans as well as the fact that they each represented one of the four provinces of Ireland.

O'Hegarty, Seán (1881–1963)

Born in 1881, Seán O'Hegarty played a major part in the organising of the final chapter in the War of Independence. He became OC Cork No. 1 Brigade after the death of Terence MacSwiney. A book on his life, written by his nephew Kevin Girvin, was published in 2007. While many fine books have been written about MacCurtain and MacSwiney, the stories of Seán O'Hegarty and Denis Barry and their involvement have until now been largely ignored. In Denis Barry's last letter to his family he singled out Seán O'Hegarty 'who did a true friend's part during my stay in Newbridge'.

Biographical Notes

Ó Mórdha, Seán (1893–1951)

Born in 1893 in the Model Cottages in Cork, he later moved with his family moved to Anne Street. He qualified as a teacher in 1913 and joined the Gaelic League when he returned to Cork after attending teacher training in Dublin. He taught in the North Monastery School, as did his brother Dan. He was a well-known and respected mathematician and joined Sinn Féin in 1919. He was elected as secretary of the Cork Comhairle Ceanntair of Sinn Féin and wrote the letter instructing the Cork TDs to vote against the Treaty. He took no active part in the Civil War. He remained a teacher until 1951 when he died at the age of fifty-seven years. Seán was also chairman of the Cork Library Committee from 1939 until his death. His picture is displayed in the Local History Department in the City Library.

O'Sullivan, Andrew (died 1923)

A native of Cavan, Andrew O'Sullivan was arrested along with many others during the Civil War and went on hunger strike in Mountjoy Jail. Having fasted for forty days he died on 22 November 1923. He was the first to be buried in the Republican Plot in the cemetery at Goold's Hill, Mallow.

Pearse, Patrick (1879–1916)

Born in Dublin in 1879, Pearse was educated by the Christian Brothers and at the Royal University where he studied Law and Arts. He joined Conradh na Gaeilge in 1895. He joined the Irish Republican Brotherhood in 1913 and was elected to its Supreme Council. He was Commander-in-Chief of the forces of the Irish Republic during the Easter Rising of 1916. After the surrender he and his brother Willie were executed by the British for their part in the Rising.

The Unknown Commandant

Plunkett, Count George (1851–1948)

Born in 1851 he was elected TD for Roscommon in 1917. He was appointed Minister for Foreign Affairs in 1919 and was a delegate to the Paris Peace Conference. His son, Joseph Mary Plunkett, a signatory of the Proclamation of the Republic in 1916, was executed by the British after 'The Rising'. He died in 1948 aged ninety-seven years.

Wallace, Nora & Sheila

Nora Wallace, Brigade communications officer Cork No 1 Brigade, and her sister Julia, known by her friends as Sheila, were shopkeepers in Brunswick Street (now St Augustine Street). They had strong Republican beliefs and their shop was the centre for passing information between the various units within the brigade area. The British believed that a tunnel existed between their shop and the Queens Old Castle drapery store. Colonel Higginson, Military Governor, issued a closure order on the premises from 14 May 1921 under Martial Law which was in force in Cork at that time.

Walsh, J. J. (1880–1948)

J. J. Walsh was Chairman of the Cork County Board of the GAA (shown wearing a bowler hat, second from left, back row) in the photograph of Blackrock Hurling Club 1910 on pg 25). A founder member of the Irish Volunteers in Cork, he was arrested for taking part in the Easter 1916 Rising but released from jail in 1917. Elected TD for Cork in 1918, he voted for the Treaty in 1922 despite being mandated by his party to vote against it. He was appointed Minister for Posts and Telegraphs in the Free State Government. He organised the Tailteann Games in 1924–1928. In a letter to *The Irish Times* in the 1930s he wrote of his regret at voting for the Treaty.

References

Chapter 4

P. 58 'Were not your orders to shoot on sight?', from Seán O'Hegarty by Kevin Girvan.

P. 58 'I hereby order and require . . .', Military Records.

P. 74 'Kidnapping, ambushing, killing . . .', from *Seán O'Hegarty* by Kevin Girvan.

Chapter 5

P. 94 'The Free State Government's attitude, led by Cosgrave and Mulcahy . . .', Dáil Reports.

P. 116 '. . . he would rather go to Hell with Denis Barry . . .' words spoken by Peter Golden, a first cousin of Terence MacSwiney, quoted in *The Irish Times* in 1925.

Chapter 6

P. 139 'To some who are buried there . . .', from the Republican Plot Memorial pamphlet published by the Cork No. 1 Brigade.

P. 142 'In more recent times . . .', (This matter has been reported in greater detail in Kevin Girvin's book *Seán O Hegarty*, pp. 122–125.)

Sources

Books

Andrews, C. S., *Dublin Made Me*, Mercier Press, Cork, 1979.

Coogan, Tim Pat, *Michael Collins*, Hutchinson, 1990.

Cronin, Jim, *Making Connections, A Cork GAA Miscellany*, Cork GAA County Board, 2005.

Girvan, Kevin, *Seán O'Hegarty*, Aubane Historical Society, 2007.

Henchion, Richard, *Bishopstown, Wilton, Glasheen*, published by the author, Cork, 2001.

Lankford, Siobhán, *The Hope and the Sadness*, Tower Books, Dublin, 1980.

Lawlor, Pearse, *The Burning 1920*, Mercier Press, Cork, 2009.

Murray, Patrick, *Oracles of God – The Roman Catholic Church and Irish Politics 1922–1937*, UCD Press, 2000.

Neeson, Eoin, *The Civil War in Ireland*, Mercier Press, 1968.

O'Connor, Frank, *The Big Fellow: Michael Collins and the Irish Revolution*, Clonmore & Reynolds Ltd, Dublin, 1965.

O'Donoghue, Flor, *No Other Law*, Anvil Books, Tralee, 1954.

O'Hegarty, P. S., *The Victory of Sinn Féin*, The Talbot Press, Dublin, 1954.

O'Mahony, Seán, *Frongoch, University of Revolution*, FDR Teoranta, Dublin, 1987.

The Unknown Commandant

Ó Súilleabhán, Michael, *Where Mountainey Men Have Sown*, Anvil Books, Tralee, 1965.

O' Sullivan, John L., *By Carraigdoun and Owenbue*, Ballyheada Press, Cork, 1990.

Various, *Rebel Cork's Fighting Story 1916–1921, told by the men who made it*, The Kerryman Ltd, Tralee, 1947.

Walsh, J. J., *Recollections of a Rebel*, Tralee, 1949.

White, Gerry and O'Shea, Brendan, *Baptised in Blood – The Formation of the Cork Brigade of the Irish Volunteers, 1913–1916*, Mercier Press, Cork, 2005,

White, Gerry and O'Shea, Brendan, *The Irish Volunteer Soldier 1913–1923*, Osprey Publishing, UK, 2003.

White, Gerry and O'Shea, Brendan, *The Burning of Cork*, Mercier Press, 2006.

GAA Club Publications
Ballymartle GAA Centenary Book, 1884–1984.

The Rockies – Blackrock GAA Club History.

Seán Beecher, *The Blues: A History of St Finbarr's GAA Club.*

School Project: *The Republican Plot, Cork*, Dónal Ó Muirthle, Pupil, Glasheen Boys National School, 1971 (available at Cork City Library).

Newspapers
Cork Examiner

Cork Evening Echo

Éire Nua – The Irish Nation

Freeman's Journal

Daily Sheet – Sinn Féin

Irish Independent

Irish Times, The

Kilkenny People

Index

The Unknown Commandant

Index

Index